The Explorers
of the Undersea World

General Editor

William H. Goetzmann
Jack S. Blanton, Sr., Chair in History
   University of Texas at Austin

Consulting Editor

Tom D. Crouch
Chairman, Department of Aeronautics
   National Air and Space Museum
   Smithsonian Institution

WORLD EXPLORERS

The Explorers
of the Undersea World

Richard Gaines

Introductory Essay by Michael Collins

CHELSEA HOUSE PUBLISHERS

New York • Philadelphia

On the cover A map entitled *World Ocean Floor* by Bruce Heezen and Marie Tharp, 1977

Chelsea House Publishers
Editorial Director Richard Rennert
Executive Managing Editor Karyn Gullen Browne
Executive Editor Sean Dolan
Copy Chief Philip Koslow
Picture Editor Adrian G. Allen
Art Director Robert Mitchell
Manufacturing Director Gerald Levine
Systems Manager Lindsey Ottman
Production Coordinator Marie Claire Cebrián-Ume

World Explorers
Senior Editor Sean Dolan

Staff for THE EXPLORERS OF THE UNDERSEA WORLD
Editorial Assistant Robert Green
Picture Researcher Alan Gottlieb
Senior Designer Basia Niemczyc

3 5 7 9 8 6 4 2

Library of Congress Cataloging-in-Publication Data

Gaines, Richard, 1942–
The Explorers of the undersea world / Richard Gaines.
p. cm.—(World explorers)
Includes bibliographical references and index.
Summary: Surveys the history of undersea exploration.
ISBN 0-7910-1323-5
        0-7910-1547-5 (pbk.)
1. Underwater exploration—Juvenile literature. [1. Underwater exploration.]
I. Title. II. Series.   92-45895
GC95.G35 1993   CIP
551.46–dc20   AC

CONTENTS

WORLD EXPLORERS

THE EARLY EXPLORERS

THE FIRST GREAT AGE OF DISCOVERY

THE SECOND GREAT AGE OF DISCOVERY

THE THIRD GREAT AGE OF DISCOVERY

CHELSEA HOUSE PUBLISHERS

Into the Unknown

Michael Collins

It is difficult to define most eras in history with any precision, but not so the space age. On October 4, 1957, it burst on us with little warning when the Soviet Union launched *Sputnik*, a 184-pound cannonball that circled the globe once every 96 minutes. Less than 4 years later, the Soviets followed this first primitive satellite with the flight of Yury Gagarin, a 27-year-old fighter pilot who became the first human to orbit the earth. The Soviet Union's success prompted President John F. Kennedy to decide that the United States should "land a man on the moon and return him safely to earth" before the end of the 1960s. We now had not only a space age but a space race.

I was born in 1930, exactly the right time to allow me to participate in Project Apollo, as the U.S. lunar program came to be known. As a young man growing up, I often found myself too young to do the things I wanted—or suddenly too old, as if someone had turned a switch at midnight. But for Apollo, 1930 was the perfect year to be born, and I was very lucky. In 1966 I enjoyed circling the earth for three days, and in 1969 I flew to the moon and laughed at the sight of the tiny earth, which I could cover with my thumbnail.

How the early explorers would have loved the view from space! With one glance Christopher Columbus could have plotted his course and reassured his crew that the world was indeed round. In 90 minutes Magellan could have looked down at every port of call in the *Victoria*'s three-year circumnavigation of the globe. Given a chance to map their route from orbit, Lewis and Clark could have told President Jefferson that there was no easy Northwest Passage but that a continent of exquisite diversity awaited their scrutiny.

In a physical sense, we have already gone to most places that we can. That is not to say that there are not new adventures awaiting us in the sea or on the red plains of Mars, but more important than reaching new places will be understanding those we have already visited. There are vital gaps in our understanding of how our planet works as an ecosystem and how our planet fits into the infinite order of the universe. The next great age may well be the age of assimilation, in which we use microscope and telescope to evaluate what we have discovered and put that knowledge to use. The adventure of being first to reach may be replaced by the satisfaction of being first to grasp. Surely that is a form of exploration as vital to our wellbeing, and perhaps even survival, as the distinction of being the first to explore a specific geographical area.

The explorers whose stories are told in the books of this series did not just sail perilous seas, scale rugged mountains, traverse blistering deserts, dive to the depths of the ocean, or land on the moon. Their voyages and expeditions were journeys of mind as much as of time and distance, through which they—and all of mankind—were able to reach a greater understanding of our universe. That challenge remains, for all of us. The imperative is to see, to understand, to develop knowledge that others can use, to help nurture this planet that sustains us all. Perhaps being born in 1975 will be as lucky for a new generation of explorer as being born in 1930 was for Neil Armstrong, Buzz Aldrin, and Mike Collins.

The Reader's Journey

William H. Goetzmann

This volume is one of a series that takes us with the great explorers of the ages on bold journeys over the oceans and the continents and into outer space. As we travel along with these imaginative and creative journeyers, we share their adventures and their knowledge. We also get a glimpse of that mysterious and inextinguishable fire that burned in the breast of men such as Magellan and Columbus—the fire that has propelled all those throughout the ages who have been driven to leave behind family and friends for a voyage into the unknown.

No one has satisfactorily explained the urge to explore, the drive to go to the "back of beyond." It is certain that it has been present in man almost since he began walking erect and first ventured across the African savannas. Sparks from that same fire fueled the transoceanic explorers of the Ice Age, who led their people across the vast plain that formed a land bridge between Asia and North America, and the astronauts and scientists who determined that man must reach the moon.

Besides an element of adventure, all exploration involves an element of mystery. We must not confuse exploration with discovery. Exploration is a purposeful human activity—a search for something. Discovery may be the end result of that search; it may also be an accident, as when Columbus found a whole new world while searching for the Indies. Often, the explorer may not even realize the full significance of what he has discovered, as was the case with Columbus. Exploration, on the other hand, is the product of a cultural or individual curiosity; it is a unique process that has enabled mankind to know and understand the world's oceans, continents, and polar regions. It is at the heart of scientific thinking. One of its most significant aspects is that it teaches people to ask the right questions; by doing so, it forces us to reevaluate what we think we know and understand. Thus knowledge progresses, and we are driven constantly to a new awareness and appreciation of the universe in all its infinite variety.

The motivation for exploration is not always pure. In his fascination with the new, man often forgets that others have been there before him. For example, the popular notion of the discovery of America overlooks the complex Indian civilizations that had existed there for thousands of years before the arrival of Europeans. Man's desire for conquest, riches, and fame is often linked inextricably with his quest for the unknown, but a story that touches so closely on the human essence must of necessity treat war as well as peace, avarice with generosity, both pride and humility, frailty and greatness. The story of exploration is above all a story of humanity and of man's understanding of his place in the universe.

The WORLD EXPLORERS series has been divided into four sections. The first treats the explorers of the ancient world, the Viking explorers of the 9th through the 11th centuries, and Marco Polo and the medieval explorers. The rest of the series is divided into three great ages of exploration. The first is the era of Columbus and Magellan: the period spanning the 15th and 16th centuries, which saw the discovery and exploration of the New World and the world ocean. The second might be called the age of science and imperialism, the era made possible by the scientific advances of the 17th century, which witnessed the discovery of the world's last two undiscovered continents, Australia and Antarctica, the mapping of all the continents and oceans, and the establishment of colonies all over the world. The third great age refers to the most ambitious quests of the 20th century—the probing of space and of the ocean's depths.

As we reach out into the darkness of outer space and other galaxies, we come to better understand how our ancestors confronted *oecumene*, or the vast earthly unknown. We learn once again the meaning of an unknown 18th-century sea captain's advice to navigators:

> And if by chance you make a landfall on the shores of another sea in a far country inhabited by savages and barbarians, remember you this: the greatest danger and the surest hope lies not with fires and arrows but in the quicksilver hearts of men.

At its core, exploration is a series of moral dramas. But it is these dramas, involving new lands, new people, and exotic ecosystems of staggering beauty, that make the explorers' stories not only moral tales but also some of the greatest adventure stories ever recorded. They represent the process of learning in its most expansive and vivid forms. We see that real life, past and present, transcends even the adventures of the starship *Enterprise*.

Matthew Fontaine Maury and the Blue Frontier

Perhaps the profoundest lesson to be learned from the history of exploration is humility. As humankind, deep into the third great age of exploration, contemplates the ending of one century and the coming of a new one, we find ourselves, like the members of virtually every generation before us, perhaps too quick in self-congratulation on our knowledge of the universe we inhabit. There are few unexplored places left on the planet, we tell ourselves, and our knowledge of the solar system is profound and expanding daily; each day, even the farthest reaches of the universe harbor fewer secrets from us.

Truly, there is reason to congratulate the scientists, wise men, and adventurers who have so advanced our understanding of the world we live in, but it would be unwise to forget that past generations, too, have been as confident about their mastery of geographic truths, only to have their world view shattered by some theretofore unimaginable discovery. Alexander the Great wept on the banks of an Asian river because he believed that he had conquered all the world there was to conquer; his domain was indeed immense, but constituted only a portion of the earth's territory, and today his despair seems absurd. The most learned men in Europe told Christopher Columbus that if there were new lands to be discovered in the Western

Matthew Fontaine Maury (1806–1873), the father of the science of oceanography. Maury dedicated much of his life to the accumulation and analysis of oceanographic data. The results of his prodigious efforts—Maury and his assistants scrutinized over one million ships' logs and converted the data into practical maps and charts for the use of mariners—forever changed nautical navigation and humankind's relationship to the oceans and seas.

Ocean, or a new route thereby to the fabled treasures of Asia, God would long since have revealed these to his people. It has only been in past decades that the true extent of the universe has been established, and it was not until 1992 that the Catholic church acknowledged the validity of Copernicus's theory that the earth revolves around the sun and not vice versa.

So it would be folly, as the 20th century draws to an end, for humankind to become too complacent in its understanding of the universe it inhabits, for who knows what future discoveries might shake its assumptions as profoundly as the beliefs of medieval Europeans were challenged by the discovery of a whole New World.

Indeed, though humankind's inexhaustible exploratory spirit increasingly manifests itself in the examination of the vast and distant heavens, there remains one region on its home planet where exploration is far from complete, a region that is home to more and more varied animal life than any other on earth, fascinating geologic phenomena, and the world's tallest mountains ranges and densest concentration of volcanoes—yet still remains largely unknown. The oceans, more properly perhaps than outer space, might truly be designated humankind's final frontier, for it is estimated that more is known about the lonely mountains and valleys on the dark side of the moon than about the ocean floor.

The story of the exploration of the oceans is therefore an ongoing one certain to require, in the years to come, frequent revisions and updating, for most of the great discoveries of oceanic exploration remain to be made. Though oceans cover more than 70 percent of the earth's surface, humankind, for all its pride in its mastery of the planet, has mapped less than 5 percent of the ocean floor. The voyage of oceanic exploration is therefore just beginning, and the narrative of that journey will not be completed for a very long time to come. For centuries, the oceans have been the roads to exploration; today, increasingly, they have become the uncharted regions to excite an explorer's hopes and dreams. The story of their exploration begins, as do so many tales of exploration, with maps—specifically with the maps of an American sailor who conceived the ambitious notion of charting the immense watery surface of the earth.

Although he was born and raised in the mountainous, landlocked frontier country of early 19th-century Tennessee, Matthew Fontaine Maury was destined to be the first pioneer of a new, unexplored frontier—the ocean depths. What moved this young man to leave behind the rugged territory that spawned such dusty frontier heroes as Davy Crockett and Sam Houston? Perhaps he heard the first calling of the ocean waves during the summer of 1814.

During that summer, young Matthew, at the impressionable age of eight, listened enraptured to the tales of his older brother John, who had just returned from a three-year cruise to the South Pacific with the U.S. Navy. John's tales were filled with tattooed cannibals and terrifying typhoons. Perhaps it was his brother John's death at sea 10 years later that finally drew Maury to the continent's edge and beyond in a symbolic and never-ending search for his "lost" and idolized older brother. Whatever the reasons, they were powerful enough to influence Maury, at age 19, to spurn his father's wish that he remain in Tennessee and manage the family cotton plantation. Instead, Matthew Fontaine Maury joined the U.S. Navy. Thus began the career of the man who would become the founder of the science of oceanography.

In 1825, with the help of his father's friend, Texas congressman Sam Houston, Maury acquired an appointment as a midshipman in the U.S. Navy and left Tennessee behind. His first assignment was aboard the USS *Brandywine*. During the *Brandywine*'s cruise to Europe, Maury quickly proved himself an exemplary and resourceful midshipman, for he felt utterly at home on the ocean. During his little off-duty time, Maury pored through the few volumes of navigation and astronomy aboard the ship, revealing an inclination toward scientific study and analysis that would eventually lead to a revolution in seamanship and the birth of oceanography. Even at this early point in his career, he complained about the lack of quality information on the science of seamanship. Mariners of the day relied on time-honored but crude

As a U.S. Navy midshipman, Matthew Fontaine Maury made his first ocean voyage at the age of 21 aboard the USS Brandywine *(pictured here) in 1825. During the Atlantic voyage, Maury, who had been born and raised in land-locked West Virginia, developed a deep and lasting affinity for blue-water sailing. But a tragic accident in 1839 would leave him unfit for nautical duty.*

navigational practices and their own experience and intui-
tion in sailing. Maury envisioned a more enlightened era,
when navigators could utilize scientific charts and other
data to more safely and quickly make their way across the
earth's oceans and seas.

Maury's thinking was heavily influenced by the work of
the remarkable Prussian naturalist and explorer Alexander

von Humboldt (1769–1859), who desired to "survey nature as a whole, and to produce evidence of the interplay of natural forces." Maury dreamed of surveying, like Humboldt, through scientific observation and analysis, the interplay of the oceans' natural forces as a whole, and of using the information gathered through such a survey to make man truly master of the seas.

Maury's next assignment with the navy was aboard the USS *Vincennes* on a three-year voyage around the world. Maury was exhilarated to have a chance to experience the oceans of the entire globe; he could not have hoped for a better, more exciting assignment. During the voyage, Maury closely observed the oceans and the manner in which the *Vincennes* was navigated. Maury studied the patterns of oceanic currents, the weather, the marine life, and the other characteristics of the earth's major waters. More and more, he was beginning to see the ocean as an interrelated system in which each aspect of the seas influenced all the other aspects, much as Humboldt perceived the natural world as an interrelated, interacting entity—what we would today call an ecosystem. And Maury continued to theorize about how this knowledge could be used to improve navigation.

Maury encountered a major distraction to his thoughts during a layover on the Washington Islands in the South Pacific. There, Maury was warmly greeted by Gattenewa, the chief of one of the islands' tribes, who had known Maury's brother John. The chief, by now a very old man, spoke lovingly of John, about John's bravery and their great friendship, and how they had fought together against a rival tribe, the Typee. Such was the chief's respect for the memory of John that he asked Maury to jump ship and remain on the island. He offered him the hand in marriage of his beautiful young daughter, a tribal princess, if he would stay. But Maury refused the tempting offer to remain as an honored inhabitant of the island paradise. He had other,

The great Alexander von Humboldt (1769–1869), Prussian naturalist, botanist, marine biologist, volcanologist, anthropologist, mineralogist, explorer, philosopher, and writer, was the greatest mind of his age. Characterized by philosopher Ralph Waldo Emerson as "a universal man," Humboldt's prophetic belief that all of nature was an interrelated ecosystem profoundly influenced the work of Matthew Fontaine Maury, who held similar views about the oceans and seas of the earth.

more pressing plans for his future. He thanked Gattenewa, bid him an emotional good-bye, and returned to the ship. By June 1830, the *Vincennes* was back in the United States.

Maury's next assignment was aboard the USS *Falmouth*, which would engage in a two-year patrol voyage along the west coast of South America. Maury, whose navigational studies and seamanship had not gone unnoticed by his superiors, was made sailing master of the ship. The duties of the sailing master included determining the ship's course and speed. It was also his responsibility to enter daily observations in the ship's log, such as the course taken, distance run, currents, winds, and weather encountered during the day's sailing, as well as any other information that might be of value. Maury thrived at this task, not only recording information but analyzing its significance and theorizing how it might be usefully applied.

During the *Falmouth*'s passage around the hazardous Cape Horn at the lower tip of South America, Maury witnessed an episode that confirmed his theories about the value of reliable navigational charts, none of which existed for those storm-tossed and perilous seas connecting the Atlantic to the Pacific.

As the *Falmouth* prepared to round the Cape, it was joined by a British vessel. Encountering driving storms and winds from the west, the *Falmouth* pushed away from the coast into open waters. There, the winds and storms abated and the ship accomplished a relatively easy passage around the Cape to the Pacific. The British vessel, on the other hand, hugged the coast and was twice driven back into the Atlantic, sustaining heavy damage in the process, before it successfully turned the Cape. To Maury, the incident proved that reliable data was essential to improved navigation. Had the captain of the British vessel been aware of weather patterns around the Cape, he might have avoided a dangerous, costly, and time-consuming episode that could very well have ended in disaster.

Maury had kept a detailed log during the Cape Horn passage. Using this information, he began writing an article, "On the Navigation of Cape Horn." He sent his article to the *American Journal of Science and Arts*, the most important scientific journal of the day. The article, published in July 1834, was the first ever published by an American naval officer, and it attracted considerable attention. Throughout the rest of the *Falmouth*'s voyage and after, Maury continued to collect data, which included not only his own observations but also any other information he could gather from other navigators and ships' logs.

When he returned to Tennessee in May 1834, the first thing Maury did was marry his longtime sweetheart, Ann. The second thing he did was begin to fashion all the information he had collected into a work entitled *A New Theoretical and Practical Treatise on Navigation*. It was a ground-breaking manuscript, and it was quickly made the official U.S. Navy manual for midshipmen. In the meantime, the name Matthew Maury had become quite familiar to naval authorities. He was promoted to lieutenant.

For the next three years, however, Maury was given relatively uninteresting assignments. He supervised coastal and harbor surveys and even spent some time as manager of the U.S. Gold Mine in Virginia. It was a frustrating time for Maury, who longed to return to the oceans and his blue-water studies. In October 1839, disaster struck. While traveling from Tennessee to New York on navy business, the stagecoach Maury was riding in overturned on a muddy road in Ohio. Maury's right leg was badly mangled. Maury survived a terrible ordeal as local physicians attempted to set his broken leg without anesthesia. The leg was incorrectly set and had to be rebroken and set again. Although the leg was saved, Maury was left with a shattered kneecap and a lifelong limp, which rendered him, according to navy regulations, unfit for active duty. Matthew Fontaine Maury would never again sail the oceans and seas.

It was a bitter blow to Maury. The thing he loved most had been taken away from him, his life's work apparently scuttled like a vessel that was no longer seaworthy. Permanently landlocked, Maury suffered deep anguish. It was on land, however, that Maury would discover his true life's work, work that would eventually change forever man's relationship with the oceans and seas of the earth and make the name Matthew Fontaine Maury known and revered around the world.

In June 1842, Maury received orders from the secretary of the navy to report to Washington, D.C., and assume the position of superintendent of the U.S. Navy's Depot of Charts and Measurements. As he explored the depot for the first time, Maury's accident began to seem like a fortuitous act of providence rather than a bitter episode of bad luck. For in the depot, available for Maury's inspection, were piled thousands of ships' logs, deposited there by mariners over the years. In these logs were recorded information about virtually every square foot of the major waters of the earth—information Maury had long craved but would have had difficulty obtaining even had he spent every hour of his entire life at sea.

Maury immediately hired a battalion of assistants to begin collecting, organizing, and statistically analyzing the data contained in the logs. Each assistant was assigned a five-degree square of ocean and charged with the laborious task of wading through the logs and recording and analyzing all the pertinent nautical information for that particular five degrees of water. A comprehensive chart began to emerge. On the chart, the oceans and seas were broken down into five-degree squares that displayed wind and ocean currents; weather conditions; water temperature; water depth (if it was known); the presence of reefs, out-

The U.S. Navy Depot of Charts and Measurements and the Naval Observatory in Washington, D.C. In 1842, Maury was made superintendent of the depot and the observatory. From here, Maury coordinated the ongoing oceanographic reconnaissance and the statistical analysis of the voluminous resulting data that would be rendered into his revolutionary navigational and bathymetric charts and maps.

Maury collected and analyzed data from the ships' logs of mariners from around the world to produce charts such as this one—a hemispheric diagram of prevailing winds. Such charts allowed mariners to utilize the winds to their fullest extent and to avoid areas of contrary and dangerous meteorological trends.

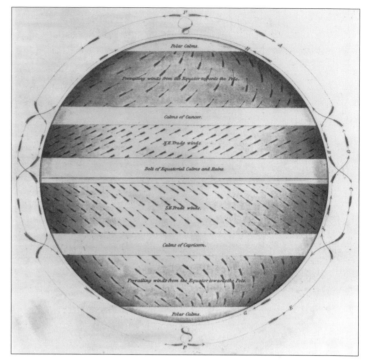

croppings of rock or sandbars (if it was close to the shoreline); the pattern of activity of sea life (such as whales) in the area, and any other available information for that particular small segment of ocean or sea.

Maury soon became obsessed with gathering new data for his charts. The logs he first encountered in the depot varied in the quantity, quality, and content of information they contained. Some mariners kept detailed logs; others were very sketchy. Maury designed his own standard log to be distributed to all U.S. Navy navigators and sea captains, thus ensuring the type and quality of data he would receive when the logs were returned to the depot after a naval voyage. This was done easily enough; the navy high command simply issued orders for U.S. Navy sailors to use the standardized logs and distributed them throughout the fleet. Commercial seamen, on the other hand, were less than willing to go to the trouble of using the standard logs;

they were accustomed to doing things their own way, and the navy had no jurisdiction over them.

However, when the first editions of Maury's charts were published in 1847 and reports of their phenomenal success began to circulate—for example, one captain, using Maury's chart, cut 35 days off the record sailing time from the states to Rio de Janeiro—seamen everywhere began clamoring for them. At this point, Maury did a most ingenious thing. Instead of selling the charts, he gave them freely to any commercial seaman who requested them, provided that the seaman also accepted one of Maury's standardized logs and agreed to fill it in and return it to the depot for analysis. Thousands of standardized logs began pouring into the depot, where their data was quickly analyzed and added to the charts. In this manner, by 1853, Maury was able to issue a series of constantly updated charts that revolutionized navigation on the high seas, making it safer, faster, and more economical than ever before.

Maury had by now acquired an international reputation. In 1853 he was instrumental in organizing the International Maritime Meteorological Conference in Brussels, Belgium. Ten nations, including the United States, Great Britain, France, and Russia, sent representatives to the conference, a remarkable occurrence in itself, because a number of these nations—such as the United States and Great Britain—were powerful and bitter rivals on the high seas. Despite initial resistance and international rivalries, Maury was able to convince the 10 nations to adopt the use of his standardized log, known simply as the *Abstract Log*, and to share the information gathered. All of this data would be added to Maury's charts as well. Now, the ships of virtually the entire seagoing world were employed in Maury's nautical reconnaissance. Even the great polymath Humboldt, Maury's idol and inspiration, had never had access to such volumes of data on the workings of the natural world.

Maury's Humboldtian approach to oceanography motivated him to investigate all aspects of the oceans, including conditions in the depths and on the ocean floor. This sounding and dredging device, invented by U.S. Navy midshipman John M. Brooke, allowed Maury's oceanographers to retrieve biological and geological samples from the deepest parts of the Atlantic Ocean between Ireland and Newfoundland.

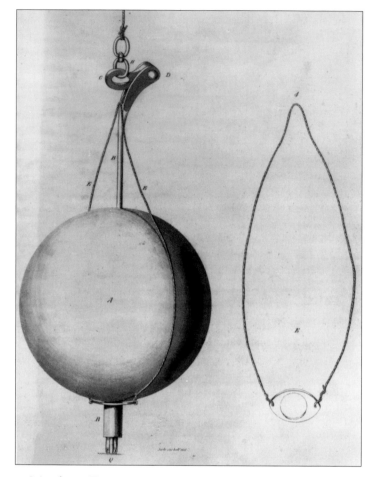

Matthew Fontaine Maury was not only interested in what occurred on or above the surface of the oceans and seas. He was just as fascinated with conditions below the surface, and particularly on the ocean floor. His endeavors to acquire data on this most mysterious of places on earth, combined with his accumulation and analysis of nautical data, heralded the birth of oceanography. Maury dispatched the first true oceanographic research vessel, the USS *Taney*, in October 1849. The *Taney* zigzagged across the Atlantic; its assignment was to determine the ocean's temperature, chemical composition, underwater currents, and marine life at varying depths and to gauge the depth of the ocean floor itself. Though some valuable data was retrieved, the mission was mostly unsuccessful, largely because of a lack of reliable depth-gauging and sample-taking equipment necessary for such research.

However, the next two research expeditions, both carried out by the *Dolphin*, achieved breakthrough results in oceanography. Utilizing a new sounding/dredging device invented by Naval Academy graduate John M. Brooke that could simultaneously measure the depth of the ocean floor and reliably collect and hold samples from the floor during retrieval, the researchers of the two *Dolphin* expeditions brought up the first-ever specimens of deep oceanic mud and also measured the depth of the floor of what Maury referred to as the North Atlantic Basin—a relatively thin path of ocean floor stretching from Ireland to Newfoundland. (A sounding device is basically a long measuring wire or cord with a weight on the end that is lowered from a ship until it encounters the ocean floor; a dredging device is a similar instrument lowered from a ship and intended to scoop out and hold samples from the ocean floor.)

A sample of the ocean floor was as valuable to the scientists of the mid-19th century as moon rocks to the scientists of the 20th, and Maury packaged the *Dolphin* samples with the utmost care and sent them off for analysis to prominent geologists at West Point, at Yale, and in Great Britain. Maury himself used the depth information to draw the first map of the terrain of the floor of a section of the Atlantic. The map, published in 1854, was entitled *Bathymetrical Map of the North Atlantic Basin with Contour Lines Drawn in at 1,000, 2,000, 3,000, and 4,000 Fathoms* and included ocean-floor valleys, ridges, plains, and plateaus. Maury's map would be instrumental in the laying of the first transatlantic telegraph cable in 1858.

In 1845, the great Humboldt, who was literally believed to be the world's most wise and learned man—he was called "the man who knows everything"—had published the first

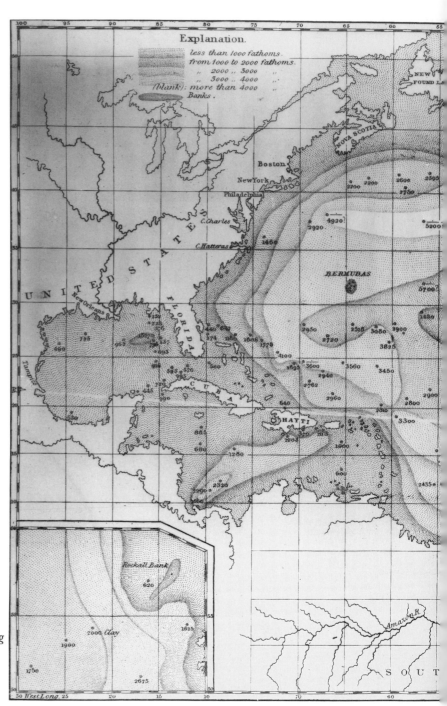

One of the first oceanic bathymetric chart. The chart, drawn by Maury, displays the varying depths of the North Atlantic Ocean floor. Measurements were acquired through the use of sounding devices—long, weighted cables that were lowered from ships until the end of the cable hit bottom.

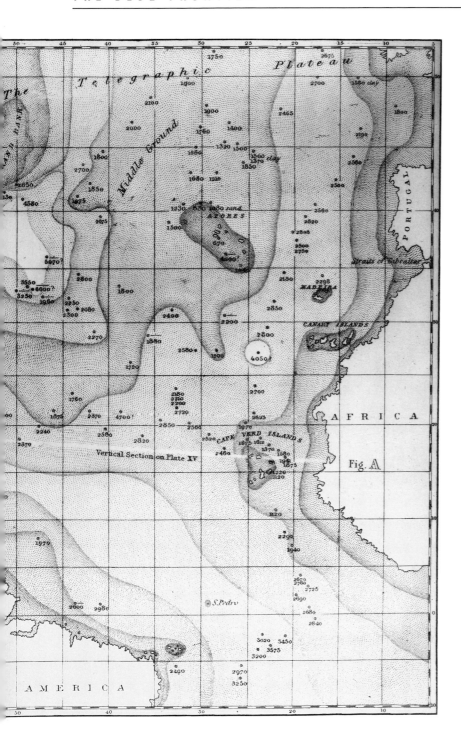

volume of his three-volume epic study of the natural world, *Cosmos*. In this massive, aptly entitled book, Humboldt strove, in his own words, "to depict the entire natural universe, all that we know of the phenomena of universe and earth, from spiral nebulae to the geography of mosses and granite rocks, in one work—and in a vivid language that will stimulate and elicit feeling."

Intended for both popular and scientific consumption, *Cosmos* was considered to be the greatest written work on the natural sciences yet produced by humankind, and its publication was the most celebrated event in the history of the printed word. It was published around the world in numerous languages, and for years, despite the considerable expense of the huge volume, which included hundreds of color plates of flora and fauna, copies literally disappeared from booksellers' shelves the moment they were placed there.

Matthew Fontaine Maury had long dreamed of writing a similar book—a *Cosmos* of the oceans and seas, for he perceived the oceans, just as Humboldt perceived the natural universe, as a single interrelated system, and he wanted to communicate his ideas, supported by the voluminous data he had acquired over the years, in a volume that would be accessible to both scientists and the general public. Encouraged by the generous Humboldt himself, Maury embarked on his project, which was published in 1855. Humboldt himself suggested the title: *The Physical Geography of the Sea*.

Although it cannot be compared to *Cosmos*, as Maury's theories lacked the breadth and profundity of Humboldt's natural philosophy and theory, *The Physical Geography of the Sea* was a watershed scientific work and a huge popular success. For decades, it was regarded as the Bible of navigation and oceanography; and, like Humboldt's *Cosmos*, it was itself a great success with the general public, finding its way to household coffee tables and libraries all over Europe and the New World. Though many of its more philosophical theories would fall into disfavor and be discounted by oceanographers and naturalists in the years to come, a number of its tenets—especially Maury's concept of the ocean as an ecosystem in which all of its different, multitudinous aspects, from water temperature to seasonal whale migrations to oceanic currents to weather patterns, contributed and depended upon all others—are accepted and essential principles of oceanography today. We know that the disruption of one of these elements can lead to a chain reaction of disruptions that can result in disastrous consequences in the balance of an ocean's ecosystem and its natural health, which in turn can have disastrous effects on humankind.

The Physical Geography of the Sea marked the culmination of a remarkable career in which one man forever changed humankind's relationship with the seas and oceans of the planet. Few men in history have had such a widespread and positive influence on the practical affairs of their fellow humans. Maury, now a world-famous figure, dined with presidents and royalty and was presented with a set of silver medals by the pope. By the time his scientific career was interrupted by the outbreak of the American Civil War, Maury, who had not been aboard a sailing vessel in more than 20 years, had become known as "the Pathfinder of the Seas."

Bathybius

The success of the two *Dolphin* expeditions in retrieving matter from the deep ocean floor and the publication of Maury's *The Physical Geography of the Sea* had a particularly electrifying effect on naturalists and biologists of the time. Humans had long wondered what kind of creatures—if any—inhabited the deepest parts of the seas and oceans. Were the deeps teeming with alien aquatic life-forms, or were they simply silt and seaweed graveyards, strewn with sunken ships and the skeletons of dead whales and doomed mariners? Early seagoers feared that the deeps were populated by fantastic sea monsters, and over the centuries fishermen in various parts of the world occasionally would bring up some bizarre-looking, never-seen-before creature that would be presumed to be an inhabitant of the abyss that had strayed upward for one reason or another.

Naturalists and biologists who studied marine plants and animals, soon to be known as marine biologists, began attempting to dredge the sea bottom for specimens of life during the late 18th century, but their efforts were restricted to relatively shallow waters. During the 1830s the Englishman Edward Forbes, Jr., dredged up sea life from waters of a depth of about 1,800 feet around the British Isles and in the Mediterranean Sea. Not long afterward, the English explorer James Clark Ross brought up a variety of aquatic specimens from a depth of 2,400 feet.

As dredging and sounding equipment improved, primarily through the work of Matthew Fontaine Maury—Maury died in 1873 in Virginia—specimens from much deeper areas of the ocean floor were brought to the surface.

Midshipmen assist an oceanographer in preparing a dredging and sounding device for use aboard the Royal Navy's HMS Challenger. *The* Challenger *voyage, launched in December 1872, was the first global oceanographic research expedition.*

On one of the *Dolphin* expeditions, a sample of fossilized marine life from a depth of three and a half miles had been retrieved. By the time of Maury's death, most marine biologists believed that the ocean floor was covered with an organism known as bathybius. A clear, slimy substance, samples of bathybius had been brought up by ocean-floor dredges conducted in the 1860s, during the laying of the first transatlantic telegraph cable. Marine biologist Thomas Henry Huxley, a close friend of the famed naturalist Charles Darwin and an early supporter of Darwin's theory of evolution, discovered bathybius while he was analyzing these deep-sea oozes. Huxley noticed a clear, jellylike substance in the jars of preserved ooze sent to him for examination. Scrutinized under a microscope, Huxley noted that the stuff had no organs, no spine, no brain, and no nervous system. He presumed that this was the most primitive life-form on earth, the basic primordial slime from which, according to Darwin, all other life-forms had originally emerged and then evolved. The over-enthusiastic Huxley based his conclusion on his "observation" that the bathybius had an "infinite capacity for improvement in every conceivable direction." Quite an assumption to make about a jar of mud, but to Huxley, the lack of a single lifelike characteristic implied that the stuff could potentially develop into any of thousands of life-forms. Bathybius, Huxley believed, was the slimy bottom rung of nature's evolutionary ladder.

The discovery and "identification" of bathybius fired the imaginations of marine biologists all over Europe and America. Clearly, with the deep-sea dredging equipment now available, new marine biology–oriented research expeditions were called for.

In 1868, two British marine biologists, William B. Carpenter and Charles Wyville Thompson, petitioned the Royal Navy for the use of one of their vessels for a research expedition. Carpenter, a highly respected naturalist who was vice-president of Britain's prestigious scientific body,

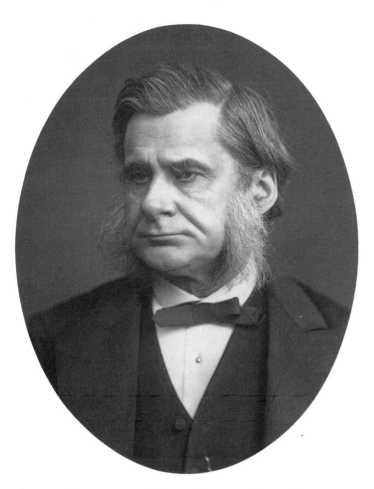

Marine biologist Professor Thomas Henry Huxley, who bore an uncanny resemblance to modern-day film and TV star Walter Matthau, was the discoverer of bathybius. Brought up from the floor of the Atlantic during the laying of the first transatlantic telegraph cable, bathybius, a clear, viscous ooze, was thought (incorrectly) to be the primordial matter from which all life on earth eventually evolved.

the Royal Society, used his influence to have the petition reviewed. The Admiralty approved the request and granted Carpenter and Thompson two weeks' use of the HMS *Lightning*, an ancient paddle steamer that was anything but lightninglike. The ship was provided with a small crew and the necessary dredging equipment, including a "donkey engine"—a motorized winch to haul in the dredging line from the depths.

The two weeks that the *Lightning* spent plying the seas around the British Isles in late August and early September were unusually stormy for that time of year, and Thompson and Carpenter spent much of their time huddled in leaky

One of the ocean-floor dredging devices used during the Challenger *expedition. Lowered by motorized winch to the ocean floor, the dredge would be dragged along slowly until it was full; it would then be hauled in and its contents evaluated.*

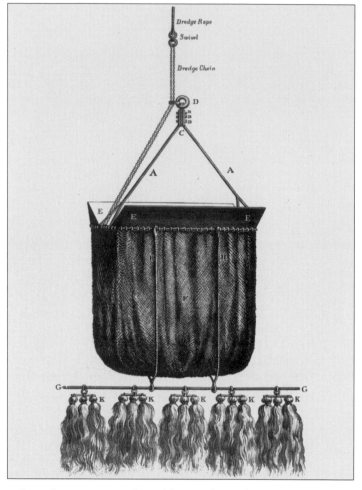

cabins listening to the old vessel creak and moan ominously as it was tossed about by the high seas. Nevertheless, the weather cleared long enough for some soundings and dredgings to be taken. One of the most important discoveries made during the voyage was that at the lower depths there were large pockets of water where the temperature changed, and these pockets were discrete and did not flow into one another. Even more important, Thompson and Carpenter learned that the type of deep-sea life varied according to water temperature.

Thompson and Carpenter managed only a few dredges into the relatively shallow seas around the British Isles during the *Lightning*'s brief voyage, but the expedition was deemed a smashing success by the Admiralty. Two similar but more extensive expeditions were dispatched in 1870 and 1871. These were also successful. Now, Carpenter, Thompson, and other members of the Royal Society and the British scientific community began lobbying the Admiralty for a full-scale, global deep-water reconnaissance to bring to the surface "the treasures of knowledge which lie hid in the recesses of the ocean."

The British prime minister William Gladstone, a good friend of Carpenter's, added his considerable political weight to the call for a round-the-world research voyage. The Admiralty acquiesced, and preparations began for the most extensive oceanographic research expedition yet attempted. Other major sea powers were launching or preparing to launch major oceanographic expeditions. As the Royal Navy had no intention of being upstaged in this new scientific arena by any of their international rivals, they outfitted their expedition to the fullest, with the best equipment and personnel available.

The HMS *Challenger*, a 2,300-ton, 226-foot-long, 30-foot-wide corvette with a 1,200 horsepower auxiliary engine, was assigned to the expedition. The *Challenger* expedition would have a crew of 240 men. It would be equipped with all the latest and best sounding and dredging equipment, including an 18-horsepower steam winch on a specially built platform on the main deck for the dredge line. A laboratory cabin was constructed on the main deck. All but 2 of the ship's 18 cannon were removed to make more room for scientific equipment and supplies, including 144 miles of hemp rope and 12 miles of wire line for sounding and dredging, sinkers, nets, a small library, hundreds of miscellaneous scientific instruments, and barrels of alcohol to preserve samples and specimens.

The complicated dredging and sounding setup aboard the Challenger. At the lower right is the motorized winch, or "donkey engine," used to lower and reel in the dredges and sounding lines. The process of dredging the ocean bottom for samples was laborious and slow, often taking all day and lasting well into the evening.

Captain George S. Nares would command the vessel, with Lieutenant Thomas Tizard as chief navigator. Charles Thompson was chosen by the Royal Society to head the scientific complement, which included Canadian naturalist and medical student John Murray and Scottish chemist John Young Buchanan, both of the University of Edinburgh.

The *Challenger* sailed from Portsmouth on December 21, 1872, and set a course for the Canary Islands, located in the Atlantic off the northwest coast of Africa. On the morning of February 26, after the ship had left the Canary Islands behind and headed west for Bermuda, the *Challenger* furled its sails, held itself steady into the wind with the auxiliary steam engine, and for the first time the winch lowered the dredge into the depths.

Then a scene that was to become familiar to all on board unfolded. The ocean floor at this initial location was 3,150 fathoms below (a fathom is six feet), and thus the *Challenger*'s first dredging attempt was over a half mile deeper than any other probe yet attempted. It took over an hour and a half for the dredge to hit bottom; often it would take much longer. Once the dredge had found the ocean floor, it would be slowly dragged along for most of the day. In the late afternoon, the winch motors would be restarted, and the marine biologists would wait impatiently, sometimes for up to four or five hours, for the noisy, laboring machine to haul its yield back to the surface.

Full darkness would have fallen by the time the dredge reappeared, and its contents would be examined by the light of the deck lamps. Sometimes the dredge yielded only pounds of clay or mud. At other times, it would reappear laden with flopping, squirming, wriggling sea creatures. Occasionally, truly unearthly creatures were retrieved from the ocean depths, creatures so strange looking that the entire crew would gather on deck to gape at them under the lights. There were gigantic sea worms, odd crustaceans, eels, jellyfish that looked like exotic, blossoming flowers, colorful sea anemones, huge clams, and, from the deepest ocean trenches, fish that actually glowed with their own source of light or fish with huge eyes at the end of stalks. In a state of near rapture, the marine biologists would remain on deck through the night, examining creatures that human eyes had never before seen.

This scenario was repeated over 300 times during a period of three and a half years as Captain Nares piloted the *Challenger* across the oceans and seas of the globe. It was often a grueling and arduous voyage, taking the marine biologists and the ship's crew from the shark-infested Caribbean tropics to the iceberg-jammed waters of the Antarctic Circle. By the time the *Challenger* returned to port in England in May 1876, the ship had traveled 68,930 miles. Seven crew members had been killed in accidents or had died of disease; others, bored with the slow pace of the voyage, had jumped ship in Australia.

The expedition had been an unprecedented success nevertheless, the greatest scientific journey yet engaged in

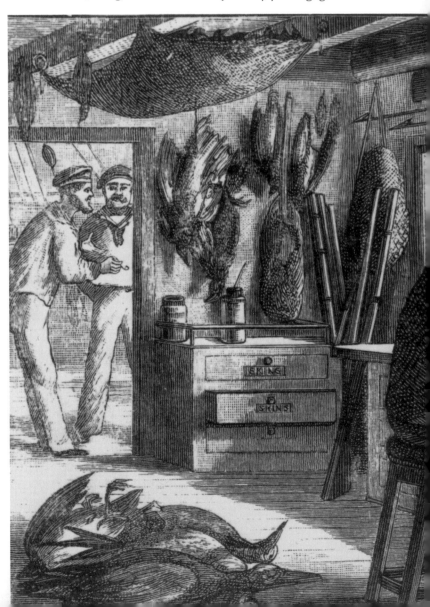

by humankind. The *Challenger* returned to England with a
wealth of information that spanned the entire spectrum of
oceanography, from marine biology to the geology of the
ocean floor and from the chemistry of the ocean's waters to
its currents and temperatures. On the biological front,
Thompson and his assistants returned to terra firma with
over 13,000 different specimens of sea animals and plants,
1,441 water samples, and hundreds of bottles of preserved
sea-floor ooze. They had also learned that animal life,

*The laboratory constructed
on the deck of the* Challenger
*transformed the ship into a true
research vessel, allowing marine
biologists, chemists, and other
scientists to immediately begin
analyzing samples instead of
packing them away for later
study by specialists on land.*

*One of the 40 "accumulators"
used during the* Challenger
*expedition. The accumulators
were used as sounding devices;
attached to the end of a long cable,
the devices were heavy and constructed to allow the currents to
flow through them so that they
could be dropped straight down to
the ocean floor and thus provide
an accurate depth measurement.*

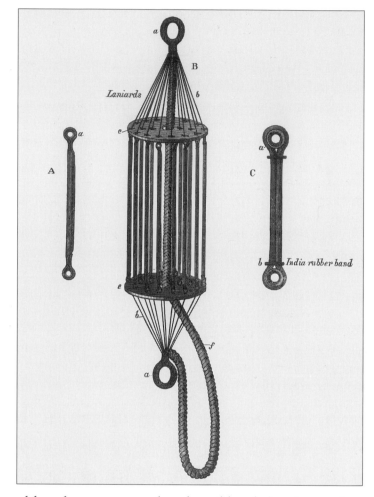

although rare compared to the wild and abundant variety
of life in shallower waters, did exist in extremely deep
waters as well, which was contrary to established scentific
opinion at that time. The *Challenger*'s hydrologists and
chemists had discovered a significant difference in temperature in the deep waters of certain sections of the
eastern and western Atlantic, causing Captain Nares to
speculate that the Atlantic's floor was divided down the
middle by an underwater mountain chain that separated
the cold southern polar waters flowing into the Atlantic
Ocean from the warmer waters around the coast of Europe

and Africa. They received readings indicating that the oceans featured strictly defined temperature layers and currents with a variety of salt content in various areas, indicating that there were major currents flowing north and south as well as east and west.

The expedition's oceanographers had maintained a steady, periodic schedule of soundings, which, when finally charted, formed the first extensive—though sketchy—topographical map of the ocean floors. They had sounded some of the deepest parts of the oceans, including the 35,810-foot abyss in the Mariana Trench, henceforth known also as the Challenger Deep, a gaping underwater canyon in the western Pacific and the deepest point on earth known to humans. This information was but a tiny portion of the massive amount of oceanographic data collected by the *Challenger* expedition.

However, among all the data and all the samples of sea life retrieved from the deeps, no sign of bathybius had been found. Rather, the marine biologists had learned that there was no such organism. In 1875, as the ship was sailing for Japan, the chemist Buchanan had noted that there was indeed what looked like bathybius slime in some of the jars of specimens that had been taken earlier in the expedition and preserved in alcohol. However, Buchanan also quickly

A sample of the North Atlantic Ocean floor dredged from a depth of 450 fathoms by the Challenger. Culled from deep sea "Pteropod Ooze," it consists primarily of mollusk and marine rhizopod (a large, creeping protozoan) shells.

Prince Albert of Monaco studies marine specimens in his private laboratory. The prince, a marine biologist in his own right, personally financed oceanographic research expeditions following the phenomenal success of the Challenger *excursion.*

perceived that there was no slime in the jars that had been preserved in seawater. Buchanan became very suspicious and conducted some simple chemical tests. He found the "bathybius" to be nothing more than a substance produced by mixing seawater and alcohol and letting it sit for a long time. When the matter was reported in the scientific journal *Nature*, an embarrassed Huxley, the discoverer of "bathybius," quickly recognized and apologized for his mistake. So much for the primordial Darwinian slime.

But the success of the mission rendered the search for and concept of bathybius obsolete. In order to organize, analyze, and classify the reams of data and the thousands of plant, animal, geologic, and water samples, the Challenger Expedition Commission was formed, and the specimens were crated and dispatched far and wide to an array of noted scientists. The distinguished American naturalist Alexander Agassiz of Harvard University received hundreds of different types of sea urchins, which took him over four years to sort and classify. (By the time he was finished, he expressed a desire never to see another sea urchin and wished the entire species extinct.) The first results of the monumental project were published in a large volume in 1880; the 50th and final volume was published in 1895. Even Alexander Humboldt and Matthew Fontaine Maury would have been astonished and delighted at this ocean of interrelated data.

Other seagoing nations, eager to share in the success of the British, launched their own oceanographic expeditions. Russia, Italy, Germany, France, Norway, and Monaco all joined in; Albert I, the prince of Monaco, considered oceanography to be his hobby, and he financed and outfitted his own expedition. The most productive of the post-*Challenger* expeditions, however, were undertaken by the United States and led by Alexander Agassiz, despite his dislike for sea urchins.

Sailing aboard the steamer *Blake* and then the USS *Albatross*—the first ship designed and built specifically for oceanographic research rather than converted from a military vessel—Agassiz covered more than 100,000 miles of ocean, and his research added greatly to the already voluminous information gathered by the *Challenger* expedition. One of the more significant discoveries made by Agassiz was a large range of underwater mountains in the eastern Pacific Ocean that he named the Albatross Range.

By the end of the 19th century, it was becoming clear that surface oceanography—that is, the use of probes, nets, lines, and dredges from the decks of ships—had been utilized to its fullest practical extent. Oceanographers now yearned for a way to more closely explore the environment beneath the ocean's waves. In order to fully understand the deeps, humans needed to descend into those deeps themselves.

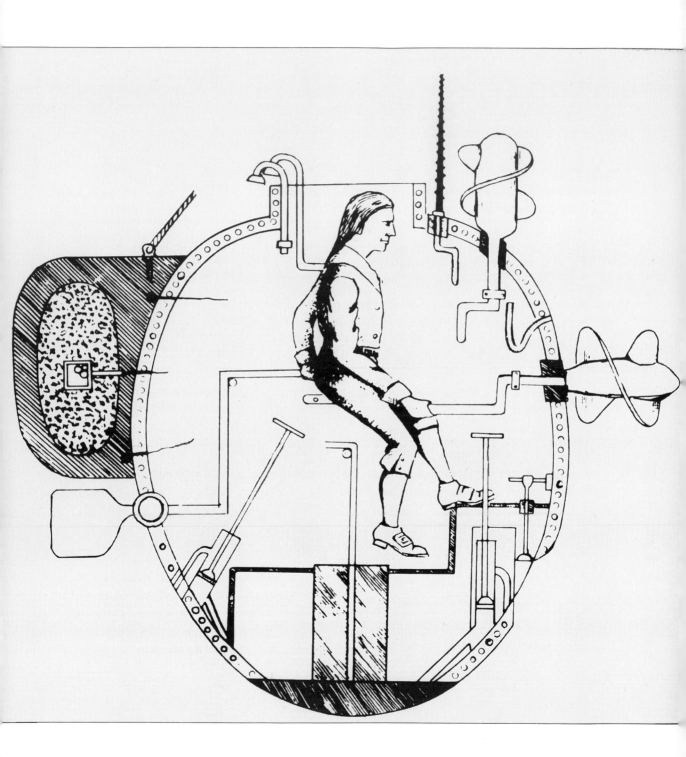

Nemo's Legacy

According to *Webster's Ninth New Collegiate Dictionary*, the word *submarine* dates back to 1703 and is defined as a "vessel that operates underwater; or, specifically, a warship that can operate on the surface or underwater." But the concept of a manned underwater vessel dates back much further. Leonardo da Vinci, the famed 15th- and 16th-century Italian artist, engineer, and inventor, envisioned such a craft during his remarkable career and even designed a prototype, but Leonardo, "on account of the evil nature of men," refused to divulge his design. Leonardo was as prophetic and prescient in his understanding of the human condition as he was in his knowledge of engineering and technology and its future potentials, for as history and *Webster's* definition attest, *warship* is the operative word when the development of the submarine is discussed, and the vessel has been used primarily as an engine of destruction rather than one of exploration and research. Nevertheless, when it has not been engaged in warlike activities, the submarine and other manned submersibles have proven to be the primary means by which humankind has been able to truly explore the world beneath the surface of the oceans and seas.

The first truly operative submarine was built by the Dutchman Cornelis Jacobszoon Drebbel in 1620. His vessel was constructed of wood reinforced by iron bands and waterproofed with leather coated by grease. It reportedly was propelled by 12 oarsmen—the oars protruded through watertight leather seals—and could carry additional passengers. It could also reportedly remain submerged for

The famous submarine the Turtle, designed and built by Yale College graduate David Bushnell just prior to the revolutionary war. Note the two hand-cranked propellers in front; one to assist submerging, diving, and turning and one for forward movement; the steering rudder in the rear; the two manual ballast pumps, one standing upright to the right and in front of the pilot and one set at an angle behind him; and the hand-operated drill atop the sub, intended to be used to drill holes in the hulls of British warships.

An engraving of the ill-fated Englishman John Day's 50-ton submarine, the Maria, *launched in 1774. During its first dive, in the Atlantic, the* Maria, *which carried 30 tons of rock as ballast, sank like a rock with Mr. Day aboard and was never seen again.*

several hours through the use of a "secret" substance called grandly and mysteriously by Drebbel "quintaessentia," which removed the poisonous carbon dioxide exhaled by its passengers. Common soda ash has the property of absorbing carbon dioxide, and some form of this substance was probably Drebbel's "quintaessentia." Despite the apparent success of his invention, Drebbel's attempts to sell it to the tradition-steeped, conservative Royal Navy were a failure. Nevertheless, by all accounts it seemed that the thing actually worked to a limited degree.

The Englishman John Day was not so successful. In 1772, Day built a small submarine that he claimed could remain submerged for 12 hours at a depth of 30 feet. Day convinced some London investors to build a larger model of his original vessel that might dive deeper and stay submerged longer. In June 1774, this vessel, christened the *Maria*, made its first test dive. Day intended to remain submerged for 24 hours at a depth of 300 feet. The *Maria* was loaded with more than 30 tons of rock as ballast; the rocks would submerge the vessel and then be jettisoned when Day was ready to surface. On the afternoon of June 20th, Day was sealed into his submarine with a candle, a clock, and a supply of biscuits. Thus equipped, Day and the *Maria* disappeared beneath the waves of the Atlantic forever. Neither submarine nor submariner were ever seen again. Search-and-rescue attempts were conducted for weeks, but by then Day had undoubtedly run out of air and biscuits.

The first truly noteworthy and documented breakthroughs in submarine technology were accomplished by David Bushnell, an American colonist and amateur engineer. Bushnell's creation, the famous *Turtle*, included innovations that became standard elements of submarine technology and remain so to this day. The *Turtle* used seawater for ballast, filling two tanks within the vessel in order to submerge and pumping out the seawater to rise and surface. The *Turtle* also featured a hand-cranked propeller in front, a steering rudder in the rear, and a small prominence atop the vessel equipped with a waterproofed window that rose above the surface—known as a conning tower. The *Turtle* could remain submerged for about half an hour.

Just as Leonardo had predicted, no sooner had a viable submarine been built than it was employed in a warlike manner; during the American Revolution, George Washington attempted to use the *Turtle* to sink a British frigate by having the *Turtle* creep up beneath the ship and attach an explosive charge to its hull. The mission, however, was a failure; the hull of the well-built ship was too sturdy for the *Turtle* men to drill through and attach their bomb. The British navy eventually sunk the pesky *Turtle*.

The development of the submarine progressed sporadically through trial and error during the latter part of the 19th century and the early decades of the 20th. The error aspect of this process was often fatal to the submariners involved, but this did not prohibit further research and experimentation. War was the primary motivating factor—crude submarines were used destructively but rather haplessly during the American Civil War—but popular literature, surprisingly, played a major role as well.

In 1870, the publication of the classic science-fiction novel *Twenty Thousand Leagues under the Sea*, by the uncannily prophetic French writer Jules Verne, inspired submarine builders and would-be submarine builders throughout Europe and the United States. Verne's novel was about a fantastic submarine, the *Nautilus*, and the undersea adventures of its monomaniacal inventor, Captain Nemo, who piloted his monstrous vehicle around and beneath the earth's waters primarily for the purpose of destroying other seagoing vessels. Nemo's *Nautilus* was the ultimate submarine; it was swift and highly maneuverable underwater, it had its own mysterious and economical power source—eventually revealed within the novel as electricity powered by seawater—and inexhaustible air supplies, living quarters for a large crew, and a hull strong enough to withstand water pressure at even the deepest parts of the ocean. The *Nautilus* could remain submerged for extended periods. It also had immense destructive capabilities, making it the scourge of the seas.

With the *Nautilus* in mind and war on the horizon, early 20th-century designers and engineers began to solve the problems that had plagued submarines thus far. Steam and gasoline replaced manpower as a source of propulsion, and they in turn were replaced by a combination of electricity and diesel fuel. Contours were reshaped for greater speed and hulls strengthened to withstand the pressure of greater depths. More practical air-supply and fresh-water supply systems were developed so the new, larger vessels might carry more men and remain submerged for longer periods, and innovations in ballast, rudders, and side-fin rudders, or diving planes, improved vertical and horizontal maneuverability. Reliable compasses, gyroscopes (a type of nautical compass), the periscope, and finally, the invention of sonar and radar improved navigation and visibility. And, of course, the torpedo, the most devastating weapon of war at sea, was developed and perfected. By the outbreak of World War I, submarines, and especially the terrifying

In this illustration from Jules Verne's prophetic science fiction novel Twenty Thousand Leagues Under the Sea, *passengers aboard Captain Nemo's supersubmarine the* Nautilus *observe a large octopus. "We shall rise to the surface and attack him with a hatchet," Nemo declares.*

German *Unterseebooten*, or U-boats, were wreaking havoc on enemy shipping, forcing the other major nations involved in the conflict to develop their own submarine fleets. The expanded combat submarine fleets of the Germans, Japanese, British, and especially the Americans played the pivotal role in winning ultimate control of the seas in World War II.

Despite the death and destruction dealt by submarines during the two world wars—hundreds of ships and submarines were sent to the bottom by torpedoes, and thousands of men were dispatched to a watery grave during these years of submarine combat—certain innovations quickly proved invaluable to the more peaceful pursuit of oceanography. Echolocation, more commonly known as sonar (sound navigation ranging), was developed in order for submarines to detect other, unseen enemy subs. Echo-

location is the same technique used by dolphins and other creatures, such as bats, to locate objects. A sound pulse is emitted; in the case of a dolphin or submarine, the pulse travels quickly because sound moves faster through water than it does through air. The pulse, when it encounters an object, then returns to the dolphin or to a receiver aboard a sub, alerting the dolphin, or submarine captain, to the

German U-boats captured by the Allies during World War I. Traveling in deadly "wolfpacks," the German subs were the scourge of the Atlantic during the early part of the conflict.

Vice admiral Hyman Rickover of the U.S. Navy emerges from his brainchild, the world's first nuclear submarine, the Nautilus. *Rickover's vision of a nuclear submarine became a reality in 1954 and revolutionized submarine technology around the world.*

object's presence and location. By the end of World War II, sound technicians had learned how to use echolocation not only to find objects but to determine their size, speed, and shape.

The end of World War II allowed oceanographers to take full advantage of sonar during the 1950s. Utilizing continued improvements in sonar equipment and techniques, oceanographers were able for the first time to draw fully detailed contour maps of the floor of the oceans. What these maps revealed astounded oceanographers and other scientists. The ocean floor, once thought to be for the most part a place of flat basins interrupted by occasional plateaus and canyons, was actually as topographically diverse as the earth's surface. There were entire underwater continents, ocean-floor volcanoes, great, gaping rifts and valleys and trenches, wide plains and towering mountain ranges.

Most startling was the presence of an undersea mountain range—first speculated upon by Captain Nares of the *Challenger* expedition—that virtually circumscribes the earth. Called the Mid-Ocean Range, or Ridge, it runs down the middle of both the Atlantic and Pacific oceans and is the tallest and longest mountain range on the planet. Such research gave not only oceanographers but geologists, seismologists, volcanologists, and other scientists an entirely new picture of the planet and its geologic origins and evolution.

Despite the advances made in submarines and submarine technology in the 20th century, the "true" submarine had yet to be built. By the 1950s, the construction of a viable true submarine seemed to exist—or had existed—as a real possibility in the minds of two men only. One of these men—the visionary novelist Jules Verne—was long dead. The other man was U.S. Navy rear admiral—and eventually admiral—Hyman Rickover.

For Hyman Rickover, the conventional diesel-electric-powered submarines of the U.S. fleet were not true submarines because they were bound to the surface by their propulsion systems. Once the batteries of these submarines had run down, they were required to surface in order to run their diesel engines and recharge their batteries. Thus, their submergence-time capabilities were limited. The true submarine, as envisioned by Jules Verne—Captain Nemo's *Nautilus*—had an inexhaustible power supply that not only allowed it to stay submerged indefinitely but supplied fresh air to the crew. Rickover believed that the fictional engine that propelled Nemo's *Nautilus* could now be made a reality through the use of the form of energy that had recently incinerated the Japanese cities of Hiroshima and Nagasaki and that had made the United States the most powerful nation on earth—nuclear energy. *(continued on page 58)*

Sea Change

According to most biologists and evolutionists, life on planet earth—including human life—originated in a marine environment. Mammals, it is believed, evolved from reptiles, which in turn evolved from amphibians, which were at one time aquatic creatures that eventually took to the land. Humankind's traditional obsession to dive beneath the oceans and seas is usually attributed to the search for food sources and products—such as pearls—of economic or symbolic value. But there is a more profound motivation behind the centuries-old quest to develop methods that might allow human divers to thrive in an underwater environment—a primal urge to return to our amphibious evolutionary origins and our true home, the watery womb of life on earth.

Humans have been diving for centuries, utilizing a variety of devices both primitive and ingenious to supply themselves with air. All of these devices—air hoses connecting the diver to the surface; diving bells; cumbersome oxygen-inflated, steel-helmeted deep-sea pressure suits—had severe limitations, however, that restricted mobility, limited the depth the diver could obtain and also the amount of time the diver could spend underwater. It was primarily through the work of a Frenchman named Jacques Cousteau—a veritable marine creature himself who has since become world-famous as a deep-sea adventurer, oceanographer, underwater filmmaker, marine biologist, and the foremost advocate of the ecological protection and preservation of our oceans and seas—that humans were finally enabled to once again freely swim, observe, and interact with the creatures of the oceans, seas, and rivers for extended periods of time.

In 1943, Cousteau, with the help of French industrialist Emile Gagnan, developed a device that would come to be known as the Aqualung. The Aqualung was put together from an automatic natural gas regulator Gagnon had developed for French automobiles, which Cousteau adapted to a mouthpiece he had created. The mouthpiece and regulator, attached by short hoses to compressed oxygen tanks strapped to a diver's back, was the first true Scuba (Self-Contained Underwater Breathing Apparatus) device, allowing humans to swim unencumbered by heavy pressure suits and helmets and untethered to surface air hoses. Gagnon's automatic regulator valve was the essential component, for it enabled divers to inhale oxygen from the tanks and then to expel exhalations out of the system and into the water in the form of carbon dioxide bubbles.

Over the years, scuba equipment has been steadily improved upon, and one has only to watch Cousteau's remarkable films to see that he and his fellow divers have indeed returned—for a period of time, at least—to an aquatic state, as they frolic with trusting whales and stroke and befriend suspicious octopi. In recent years, the visionary Frenchman has been researching the concept of actually altering the human physique itself—by surgically implanting gills, for example—to truly adapt it to an aquatic environment. Although this sounds like something from a science fiction novel, writers such as Jules Verne have proved that there is often only a matter of time and technology between science fiction and science fact.

Jacques-Yves Cousteau waves from the deck of his research vessel the Calypso. Through his development of the aqualung, his pioneering use of underwater habitats for humans, and the more than 70 popular films he has made during his career, Cousteau has done more than any other man or woman to put the human race back on intimate terms with the oceans, seas, and rivers of our planet.

(continued from page 55)

Initially, Rickover encountered considerable opposition from navy brass, many of whom felt that the idea of a nuclear submarine was not technologically feasible—or safe—because of the difficulties and the dangers of attempting to harness the immense powers of nuclear energy and then to confine them to a small, enclosed vessel that traveled, with humans aboard, in the most dangerous environment on earth. But Rickover's vision was a powerful one, as was his personality—which soon became legendary—and in 1954 the first nuclear submarine was launched by the U.S. Navy. It was christened the *Nautilus*.

Rickover's *Nautilus*, like Verne's, was a true submarine. Powered by a small nuclear reactor that was shielded from the crew, it, and the fleet of nuclear submarines that followed, quickly rendered obsolete all other forms of submarine. Its nuclear power source made it faster, allowed it to be larger, enabled it to remain submerged for months at a time, and also provided fresh water and air to the crew.

Among the navy's nuclear engineers, however, there remained doubts about the performance and safety of the *Nautilus*. The sub was put to the ultimate test in 1957, when it engaged in one of the last great voyages of discovery: a journey beneath the North Pole. Whereas the icy polar seas and the polar ice cap itself had turned back the ships of such legendary mariners as Captain Cook, James Clark Ross, and Fridtjof Nansen, the *Nautilus*, it was hoped, would overcome, or more accurately, undermine, these frozen obstacles by sailing beneath them, if, indeed, such a passage was possible, which was not at all certain.

The *Nautilus*'s North Pole expedition was led by U.S. Navy commander William R. Anderson, a veteran of the terrible submarine warfare of the Second World War. Like all the previous mariners who had attempted to sail to the North Pole, Anderson's primary concern was the ice. Unlike Cook or Nansen, however, who were confronted with the task of sailing around, over, or through the ice, Anderson's worries were focused on what lay beneath

the ice. Was there room in between the surface ice cap and the polar ocean floor for the 320-foot-long, 28-foot-diameter *Nautilus* to slip through on its way to the pole? Or would the ship and its crew become trapped and frozen in solid ice like a carp in a winter pond? Would a hard collision with the ice damage the nuclear reactor or its shield, causing loss of power or, even worse, radioactive leakage and contamination of the crew, or possibly even a massive fire or explosion? Navigating by compass and gyrocompass (a type of gyroscope) in the powerful magnetic field of the polar regions was also difficult. Would the ship become lost beneath the ice pack and unable to surface through the thick ice to allow its crew to take an astronomical reading of its position?

The Nautilus *at sea. A "true" submarine, the* Nautilus *could remain submerged for months at a time, comfortably support a crew of 105, and cruise at speeds of up to 20 knots per hour underwater.*

The first attempt by the *Nautilus* to reach the pole, via Greenland and Spitsbergen, was initiated on August 19, 1957. The attempt was a failure, although, as Commander Anderson put it, "it was one hell of an interesting cruise." The "cruise" became extremely "interesting" when both of the submarine's gyrocompasses malfunctioned just north of 87 degrees north latitude, which resulted in navigational confusion that eventually had the *Nautilus* going in circles and sailing perilously close to the shallow waters off the Greenland coast. Once he had gotten a fix on his vessel's location, Anderson prudently returned the sub to port in

Pearl Harbor. Although the attempt to reach the pole had failed, the *Nautilus* had gone farther north than any sea-going vessel in history.

A second attempt fared little better. This time, Anderson hoped to get below the ice pack by entering the Bering Strait from the Pacific, but the mission was plagued by mishaps from the start, including a fire in the engine room that could have been disastrous had the *Nautilus* been deep under the ice at the time, for the fire forced the sub to surface immediately in order to clear the smoke that was filling its interior. But what ultimately turned back the

The officers of the Nautilus *gather on the bridge to observe the approaching ice pack during the North Pole expedition of 1958. The submarine's commander, William R. Anderson, is at the far right.*

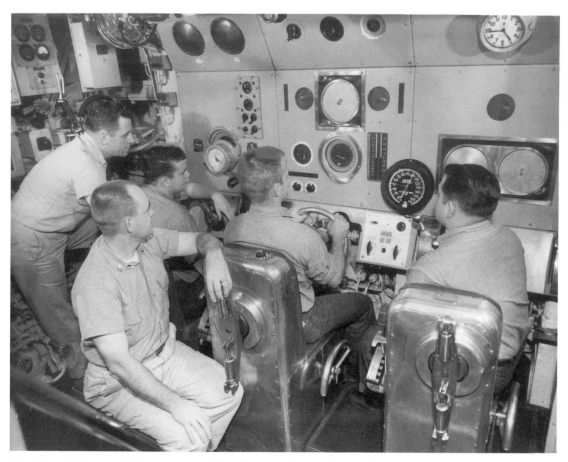

Members of the crew of the Nautilus sweat it out in the control room as the nuclear submarine maneuvers through the harrowing glacial topography beneath the ice cap on its way to the North Pole. The Nautilus made history when it passed beneath the Pole on July 3, 1958, becoming the first seagoing vessel to reach 90 degrees north latitude.

Nautilus was the traditional enemy of the Arctic mariner—ice. Commander Anderson's vessel encountered ridges of pack ice in the Bering Strait that were so large and whose undersides plunged so deep that they virtually touched the floor of the strait. The way was blocked. Again, Anderson ordered the sub back to Pearl Harbor.

Commander Anderson, in a manner reminiscent of that greatest of all mariners, Captain James Cook, who, almost two centuries earlier, had attempted three times to penetrate the Antarctic ice wall in his ship the *Resolution*, was ready for a third try by midsummer 1958. This time, the *Nautilus* eased through the Bering Strait without incident and then plunged deep beneath the north polar ice cap at a point off the coast of Alaska. Captain Cook, who had also explored these waters—he sailed virtually everywhere—and was renowned for his concern for the comfort and health of his crew, would have been astonished at the conditions within the *Nautilus*. It was warm enough for shirtsleeves. The crewmen slept on beds in small but comfortable quarters. There were bathrooms with showers; a kitchen; a dining room; game rooms and lounges; an extensive library of books and movies that could be screened during off-duty hours; there was even a jukebox and a Coca-Cola machine.

Despite the creature comforts, the expedition was as perilous as any undertaken by Cook. Any type of serious mishap below the ice would mean certain death for everybody aboard the *Nautilus*, a fact that the entire crew was well aware of. During some of the more harrowing episodes of the voyage beneath the ice, the strain on the nerves of the submariners was almost overwhelming. At certain particularly hair-raising times, the big sub was forced to nose its way through places where the ocean floor rose up into a jagged mountain range while the belly of the ice above dropped down, leaving, at times, no more than 20 feet of clearance above and below the *Nautilus*.

As the *Nautilus* edged through these perilous areas, the crew and officers would remain frozen at their stations for hours, sweating profusely, peering unblinking at their instruments or listening motionless through headphones, while Captain Anderson himself remained bent over the closed-circuit television screen on the bridge, watching intently as the ice closed in on his vessel from above and below. At these times, there would be dead silence within the submarine except for the sounds of the various instruments, the "ping" of the sonar, and the gentle hum of the engine. Nobody spoke a word unless it was absolutely necessary; usually it would be a simple number spoken by someone at an instrument panel, but a number that held a life-and-death significance. All of them waited for the sudden, jarring impact and the terrible sound of jagged ice tearing into the hull. Only when deep water had been reached once again would the sweat-soaked, emotionally and physically exhausted men relax, and nervous laughter, curses, and exclamations of relief would be heard throughout the submarine. Anderson, seeing the threatening ridges finally drop away beneath the sub, would cease his vigil and straighten up with difficulty, his back seemingly frozen into a bent-over position. On such days he would recall the deadly silent cat-and-mouse duels engaged in by enemy submarines stalking one another during the war.

On July 3, 1958, Captain Anderson prevailed over—or under—the ice, and the world's first nuclear submarine passed silently and unseen beneath the North Pole. It was silent above the ice, as well, except for the desolate polar winds; inside the *Nautilus*, once Anderson had radioed the coded message back to Washington, D.C.—"Nautilus Ninety North"—a rather boisterous party was under way. As soon as its crew could locate a large enough hole in the ice, the *Nautilus* surfaced and Commander Anderson got out and procured a large chunk of polar ice, which was kept frozen until Anderson could present it to Admiral Rickover.

Rickover was vindicated; Anderson was a national hero; and it was not long before the U.S. Navy had begun the process of converting its entire submarine fleet to nuclear power. Nor was it long before Cold War strategists realized that nuclear submarines armed with nuclear missiles could be the most stealthy and devastating weapons of war yet to be created. Today, they are the single most important strategic and tactical element of the United States's war machine. In the event of a major nuclear exchange between superpowers, only the submarines will survive with their offensive capabilities intact. The final, apocalyptic endgame will be played out beneath the oceans by these stealthy craft. (continued on page 73)

Aliens

The deep-sea submersible Alvin *surfaces following a 1977 exploratory dive to hydrothermal vents in the Galápagos Rift on the floor of the Pacific Ocean.*

In February 1977, the deep-sea submersible *Alvin* was launched on a diving expedition to explore the Galápagos Rift—a seam between spreading tectonic plates in the Pacific Ocean floor at a depth of about a mile and a half. Oceanic geochemists and geologists believed that the cracks between the moving plates—tectonic plates form the very crust of the earth beneath the continents and the oceans—would produce a phenomenon known as hydrothermal vents. These vents in the ocean floor would release hot, mineral- and chemical-rich waters from the earth's volcanic interior into the cold waters of the ocean depths. The 1977 *Alvin* expedition was the first attempt by scientists to investigate active hydrothermal vents.

The scientists aboard *Alvin* succeeded beyond their wildest expectations in locating hydrothermal vents. They also discovered something else; something totally unexpected and, initially, inexplicable. Surrounding the vents were communities of life-forms so strange in appearance and behavior that the first scientists to observe them found themselves in a state of intellectual disorientation. Animal life indigenous to the cold darkness of the deep ocean floor, well beyond what biologists had always assumed was the singular catalyst and energy source for life on earth—sunlight and photosynthesis—had been, up to this point, inconceivable. But here were thriving colonies of creatures, some of them so bizarre that it was hard to think of them as animals at all. Subsequent analysis of these organisms revealed that they were, in effect, aliens—creatures that existed outside of the previously established biological and nutritional parameters of life on this planet, part of a chemosynthetic, rather than photosynthetic, food chain that was based on energy generated by volcanic activity within the earth rather than by the sun.

Alvin, *its prow laden with a variety of research equipment, including a sample vacuum, sample basket, grasping claw, heat probe, lights, and cameras, begins a dive to hydrothermal vents a mile and a half beneath the surface of the Pacific.*

A "black smoker," or submarine chimney, vents hot, dark plumes of iron-, copper-, and zinc-laden water from a crack in the ocean floor. Heated by volcanic forces beneath the tectonic crust, the chimney smoke's temperature was a recorded 650 degrees Fahrenheit.

A thicket of hydrothermal organisms known as red-tipped
tube worms. The worms, which can grow as long as 12 feet,
have no eyes, mouth, stomach, or anus. They absorb
nourishment—molecules of bacteria—through hundreds
of thousands of tiny tentacles that cover their surface.

One of the more bizarre creatures discovered at the hydrothermal vents was a new species of siphonophore, an extremely distant relative of the Portuguese man-of-war.

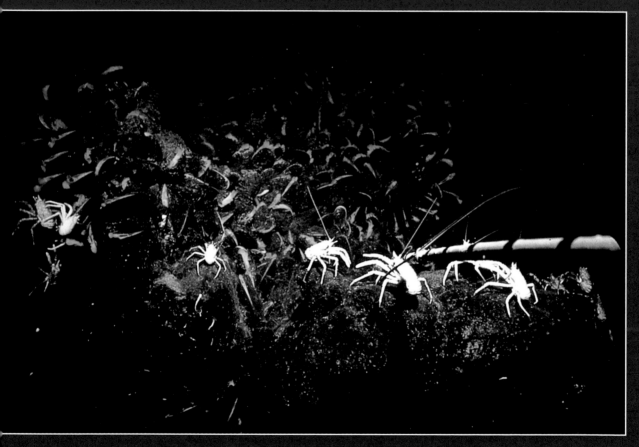

A caravan of blind brachyuran vent crabs scuttle across an outcropping of volcanic rock. The white crabs congregated by the thousands around the hydrothermal vents.

A never-before-seen species of eel slithers across a bed of sulfide sediment amid a galaxy of blue vent anemones.

An inquisitive grenadier fish inspects Alvin's
water-sampling probe. In order to see in the
sunless depths of the ocean floor, the grenadier
has developed eyes that are among the most
sensitive in the animal kingdom.

(continued from page 64)

They are true submarines in every sense of the word, just as Jules Verne and Hyman Rickover envisioned. And, like Nemo's *Nautilus*, they are the ultimate weapons of war, able to cruise the world's oceans wraithlike and unseen and to annihilate a city from some hidden vantage point deep beneath the sea. But they are not perfect. No vessel created by humans is impervious to the powers of the ocean.

On the morning of April 10, 1963, the USS *Thresher*, pride of the U.S. Navy, made a test dive about 220 miles off the coast of Massachusetts. The *Thresher* was the navy's first deep-diving nuclear submarine, a hunt-and-kill sub designed to stalk and destroy enemy subs at depths

The nuclear submarine Thresher *is launched at the Portsmouth, New Hampshire, naval shipyard on July 9, 1960. Despite the success of nuclear subs such as the* Nautilus, *and the* Triton, *which circumnavigated the globe underwater in 1960, submarine travel remained highly unpredictable and dangerous. During a test dive in deep waters off the Massachusetts coast on April 10, 1963, the* Thresher *vanished with all hands.*

The bathyscaphe Trieste *surfaces following an ocean-floor search for signs of the doomed nuclear submarine* Thresher *and its 123-man crew. The U.S. Navy turned to small, deep-diving submersibles such as the* Trieste *in the hope of ascertaining the fate of the* Thresher.

previously inaccessible to other submarines. Shortly into the test dive, the navy ship monitoring the test received a brief message from the *Thresher*: "Experiencing minor difficulties . . . Attempting to blow [surface]." That was the last anyone ever heard of the *Thresher* or its 129 crewmen. They were gone, swallowed by the ocean as irrevocably as the hapless John Day in his *Maria* almost two centuries before. The navy had not yet developed submarine rescue vehicles such as it has today, and thus all of the *Thresher*'s modern technology was about as useful to the submarine and its crew as Mr. Day's biscuits were to him.

The *Thresher* disaster was a monumental setback in the navy's plans for a nuclear submarine fleet. The navy high command was desperate to know what had happened to the *Thresher*. Most naval engineers believed that the sub had simply dived too deep and that its hull had imploded like an eggshell under the tremendous water pressure. All that was certain was that the remains of the *Thresher* and its crew lay some 8,000 feet down on the floor of the Atlantic. There was only one vessel on earth at that time that could withstand the intense water pressure at those depths—about 4,000 pounds per square inch. It was a bathyscaphe called the *Trieste*, and it was quickly summoned from its base in San Diego to search for any sign of the doomed nuclear submarine. Ironically, the *Trieste* was a vessel of pure oceanographic research rather than a military vessel, and its usefulness had long been scoffed at by the navy high command.

"Only Dead Men Have Sunken So Deep"

While the governments of the major nations were using submarine technology to blow one another's ships and subs to bits on the high seas during the two world wars, there was a tiny group of people who were building vessels that could plumb the ocean depths for purely scientific—and peaceful— pursuits. They were a remarkable group, partly inventors, adventurers, and inner-space explorers and partly naturalists, oceanographers, and marine biologists. Initially regarded by the navy as crackpots and egghead refugees from H. G. Wells's novels, they were free to engage in their oddball endeavors without interference from the military, which, during wartime, had the habit of co-opting any technology deemed useful to the war effort.

These people all had one goal in mind: to descend into the ocean's deepest and darkest depths, well below the depth capabilities of conventional submarines, to see what was down there, and to take biological and geologic samples back to the surface. They were, in a sense, astronauts of the ocean deeps, and indeed, the first bathysphere, the vessel that would carry them into the abyss, bore a remarkable resemblance to the first manned spacecraft, the Soviet Union's Vostok. This first bathysphere was constructed by the Humboldtian character Charles William Beebe of Brooklyn during the early 1930s. Beebe was

The redoubtable Swiss adventurer, Professor Auguste Piccard (right), and his copilot pose in stratospheric garb, along with family members, in front of the hydrogen balloon, designed by Piccard, that would carry the two men to a record ballooning altitude of 51,193 feet in 1931. Following his ascent into the stratosphere, Piccard and his son Jacques turned their attention to the ocean deeps.

a distinguished naturalist, ornithologist, marine biologist, and world explorer. His bathysphere, like the Soviet spacecraft, looked like nothing so much as a large cannon-ball. A hollow sphere built of heavy steel, with room for a single passenger and a tiny porthole and searchlight for viewing, its small size and spherical shape were best for withstanding the tremendous water pressure it would en-counter in the true deeps, pressure that would crush a less sturdily hulled, elongated submarine, not to mention a

diver. Beebe's capsule would be connected to a surface ship by a tether, an air hose, and a telephone line.

In 1934, off the coast of Bermuda, Beebe squeezed into his bathysphere and was lowered, much like the sounding and dredging probes of the *Challenger* expedition, into the sea by a motorized winch. Slowly he was lowered into the depths, well past the deep-dive record of any conventional submarine, and even below the depth of the oceans' deepest-diving whales. No human had ever been so far

Dr. Charles William Beebe (center), Brooklyn-born naturalist and explorer, and two associates pose with Beebe's bathysphere in November 1932. At the time, Beebe was conducting deep-dive tests of the bathysphere off the coast of Bermuda, where he had established the oceanographic research facility, Nonsuch Station.

Beebe's bathysphere, painted with the names of its sponsors, is lowered into the ocean. Passengers entered the sphere through the hatch on its right, which was then securely bolted shut from the outside. On its left are two small viewing portholes and a searchlight. In 1934, Beebe descended in the bathysphere to a record depth of 3,028 feet.

down—at least no living human—and above, on the support ship's telephone line, Beebe's crackling voice was heard to utter, "Only dead men have sunken so deep." Light faded to a complete, sunless darkness, and the temperature within the capsule dropped to just above freezing. The tether played out at 3,028 feet, and the bathysphere hung suspended in utter darkness. Beebe felt as "isolated as a lost planet in outermost space." He switched on the searchlights and peered out the porthole. His messages over the telephone line grew briefer and farther apart and then ceased altogether. The listeners above were alarmed at first, but they could hear him breathing steadily over the phone line, and they realized that Beebe was gazing out, entranced, at a world no human had ever witnessed. He remained at the window for hours. When he finally surfaced and climbed out of the cramped capsule, his exhilaration was visible on his face. He said that he felt like an astronaut who had just returned from Mars.

The name Piccard has become legendary not only among

deep-sea explorers but among all adventurers, for in their time the members of this intrepid Swiss clan explored both the heights of the earth's stratosphere and the ultimate depths of its oceans. In August 1932, after years of research and experimentation with unmanned balloons, Auguste Piccard, a mechanical engineer and physicist, along with his associate Paul Kipfer became the first humans to ascend into the stratosphere in a balloon, riding in an enclosed, pressurized aluminum sphere attached to a hydrogen balloon and reaching an altitude of 55,577 feet.

Having penetrated the stratosphere, Auguste Piccard turned his attention to the ocean depths. "So many questions, so many mysteries," Piccard was heard to say about the ocean. "It is only by going down ourselves to the depths of the sea that we can hope to clear them up." And so Piccard began building a craft that would do just that. Using much of the technology and engineering he had employed in designing the pressurized cabin for his balloon (his *Trieste*, in effect, was an underwater balloon, with a pressurized passenger sphere, much like Beebe's, attached below an expandable and deflatable tank of gasoline that served as ballast), he began constructing a deep-diving bathyscaphe in 1937. The difference between a bathyscaphe and a bathysphere, such as Charles Beebe's, is that a bathyscaphe is an untethered vehicle with a propulsion and ballast system and an oxygen supply of its own.

Piccard began work on his bathyscaphe in 1937; financed by private industry and with the help of his son Jacques, the *Trieste*, as it was christened, was breaking depth records by 1953. By the late 1950s, the *Trieste* had made so many successful dives in oceans and seas around the world and its passengers had gathered so much oceanographic information that had been previously inaccessible that the U.S. Navy had taken notice. In 1958, the U.S. Office of Naval Research purchased the *Trieste* and the services of Jacques Piccard. A plan was set in motion for the ultimate deep-ocean dive—a descent to the floor of the Mariana Trench.

The Mariana Trench is truly the abyss, a plummeting gash in the floor of the west Pacific Ocean off the island of Guam. It is the deepest, darkest place on earth, its floor lying some 36,000 feet below the ocean surface. On January 23, 1960, Jacques Piccard and navy lieutenant Don Walsh sealed themselves into the *Trieste* and began the descent. It was a gentle, seemingly endless drop into watery night. During the four-and-a-half-hour drop, the *Trieste* passed through a strata of sea life and light. At first they descended through sunlit, plankton-rich waters that were crowded with marine life. Some of the creatures were startled by the strange appearance of this craft and darted away; others were more inquisitive, peering into the bathyscaphe's port-hole with a curiosity that mirrored that of the passengers peering out.

The abundance of sea life began to thin out as the vessel sank through a dim, eerily twilit world; as they fell beyond the reach of the sun, strange, never-before-seen creatures appeared: gigantic worms and oddly angelic, luminescent ectomorphs. About three hours into the dive, the *Trieste* fell into the abyss of the trench itself, and the craft and passengers were enveloped in a darkness that was darker than any night—the utter blackness of a place where sunlight had never been. The searchlight cast a feeble light into this endless night. At four and a half hours into the dive, the *Trieste* settled gently to the floor of the trench. The searchlight had revealed no signs of life for nearly an hour. As they peered out the porthole, a profound loneliness, bordering on despair, crept over the passengers. They felt they had fallen into a truly lifeless, godforsaken place. And then, to their astonishment, a fish swam by. It looked like a flounder! It was a transcendent moment for the two explorers and for the entire community of marine biologists as well. Here, even in the most sunlight- and oxygen-deprived place on earth, there was life.

Piccard and Walsh prepared to ascend. Although neither one of them voiced their fears, it was the most nerve-

racking part of the expedition. They were resting on the floor of the deepest part of the ocean, far beyond any hope of rescue, in a tiny sphere that was enduring seven tons of pressure per square inch. Even a pinhole-sized hole in the hull would allow in a needlelike stream of water that would carry enough force to cut a hole clean through a man. And if the *Trieste*'s ascent ballast did not work, Piccard and Walsh would surely die two of the loneliest deaths ever endured by men, as their lights failed, plunging them into an all-consuming blackness, and they waited, accompanied only by their own thoughts, for their oxygen supply to run out.

But Piccard's *Trieste* gently ascended like an air bubble to the surface, just as it was designed to do, and the two

(continued on page 86)

Auguste Piccard's bathyscaphe Trieste *is prepared for a test dive in the Mediterranean Sea in 1954. The small, round passenger sphere is attached below the large, elongated tank, which would be filled with gasoline. Because gasoline is lighter than water, the tank and passenger sphere would rise to the surface when the* Trieste *purged its heavy ballast, which consisted of several tons of steel pellets.*

Aquanauts

Submersibles such as the *Trieste* and *Alvin* allow humans to explore the deeps from the (relative) safety of a mobile, life-supporting environment. But these vehicles can only remain submerged for a limited period of time; *Alvin*, for example, has an 80-hour maximum life-support capability, and its dives rarely last more than 12 hours. Nuclear submarines support scores of humans in a comfortable environment for months at a time underwater, but these subs are essentially vessels of war rather than of oceanographic research. There is, however, only a short conceptual link between the reality of mobile, if limited, underwater human-life-supporting vehicles and more permanent underwater habitats for humans.

Not surprisingly, the first seafloor habitat was established by Jacques Cousteau and the crew of his renowned research vessel the *Calypso*. In September 1962, Cousteau launched his Conshelf (Continental Shelf Station) project in the Mediterranean Sea. The habitat, named *Diogenes*, was a pressurized yellow cylinder resting on the seabed at a depth of about 40 feet. It was manned by aquanauts Albert Falco and Claude Wesly. The two aquanauts inhabited *Diogenes* for a week. Their daily routine included research excursions outside the habitat, visits from other divers, and communication via radio and closed-circuit television with various people on the surface. After a week they emerged with no physical ill-effects, but they displayed a dramatic change in their point of view of the world and humanity. As aquanaut Falco put it, "Everything is *moral* down there."

Conshelf was followed by Conshelf II, a larger, more advanced habitat known as Starfish House. Starfish House, a star-shaped life-supporting habitat that rested on telescopic legs on the floor of the Red Sea, featured sleeping quarters for five aquanauts, a fully equipped research laboratory, and a "garage" for Cousteau's submersible vehicle, the diving saucer. Deep research dives and exploratory expeditions in the saucer down the slope of the continental shelf filled the aquanauts' days and nights. At night the entire compound would be brilliantly illuminated by lights, and marine life, attracted by the light, would swarm about the area. The inhabitants of Starfish House would issue forth to mingle and interact with their neighbors. During one such interlude, the divers drew a massed attack of at least 70 sharks, forcing 3 of the aquanauts to find refuge in a shark cage built to accommodate 3 divers, while the 2 other divers fought off the sharks with cameras and lighting equipment.

In 1965, Conshelf II was followed by Conshelf III, a globe-shaped habitat situated about 350 feet below the surface of the Mediterranean. During their stay in Conshelf III, the six Cousteau aquanauts maintained radio communications with a group of U.S. Navy aquanauts—including former astronaut Scott Carpenter, who lived underwater for a record 30 days—who were inhabiting the navy's Sealab II undersea habitat in the Pacific Ocean off the coast of California. The Sealab aquanauts used a trained porpoise named Tuffy to deliver messages and tools to and from support vessels on the surface.

Both the Conshelf and Sealab experiments were unexpectedly successful and were soon followed by the establishment of similar underwater habitats, such as oceanographer Sylvia Earle's Tektite project in 1969. Although interest and funding for such projects has since faltered, many people, from oceanographers to agriculturalists to demographers, believe that underwater habitats represent the first step in the ultimate and inevitable colonization of the ocean and sea floors, and envision a day when advanced and extensive underwater farming and mining colonies and communities will utilize the vast spaces and the wealth of food and mineral resources of the deeps to relieve a desperately overpopulated planet and its starving inhabitants.

Aquanaut Dr. Sylvia Earle emerges from the Tektite 2 underwater habitat off the coast of the Virgin Islands in July 1970. Many of her friends and colleagues believe that the remarkable Earle may be the first of a new species speculated upon by Cousteau—Homo aquaticus—for she seems more at home underwater than on the land. Along with her work on the Tektite project, as well as in oceanography, marine botany and biology, and marine environmental conservation, Earle holds the record for the deepest solo dive ever made—1,250 feet.

Jacques Piccard (right) and an associate pose atop the conning tower of the Trieste *following a test dive in the waters off Guam in November 1959. On January 23, 1960, Jacques and Navy lieutenant Don Walsh descended seven miles in the* Trieste *to the floor of the Mariana Trench—the deepest place on earth.*

(continued from page 83)

men emerged to tell their tale and inform the world's marine biologists that yes, there was life even in the abyss. The *Trieste*, and a modified version of the bathyscaphe, the *Trieste II*, went on to other dives and other adventures, including locating and photographing pieces of the doomed nuclear sub *Thresher*. (The cause of the *Thresher* disaster was never fully determined. It would not be the last nuclear submarine to meet such a fate.)

Beebe's bathysphere and the *Trieste* proved that manned deep-sea exploration was indeed feasible. However, Beebe's capsule and the first *Trieste* were basically deep-sea elevators. For the most part, they went straight down and then straight up again. Deep-sea explorers craved for mobile submersibles, as these vehicles had come to be known, vessels that could withstand extreme depths and also move about at will to facilitate observation, salvage, and research. Research and development for a number of these craft was already under way as Jacques Piccard and Lieutenant Walsh sat in the *Trieste* on the floor of the Mariana Trench. Various governments and corporations were involved. A good number of these proposed craft never made it off the drawing boards because of seemingly insurmountable technical difficulties or, more often, a lack of funding. One of the first successful submersibles was the *Aluminaut*, an all-aluminum deep-diving vehicle built by the General Dynamics Corporation. The *Aluminaut* began making successful test dives in the early 1960s. At the time of his death in 1962, Auguste Piccard was at work on a submersible he called a mesoscaphe; Jacques Piccard would eventually finish his father's work, and in 1968 he piloted the mesoscaphe *Auguste Piccard* through the Gulf Stream from Florida to Cape Cod to study the current's marine life. By 1964, the famous Jacques Cousteau's *La Soucoupe*, also known as *Deepstar*, or simply "the diving saucer"—it resembles nothing so much as an underwater flying saucer—had embarked on its long career. But perhaps the most extraordinary of the early submersibles—and by far the most productive to date—was the *Alvin*.

Alvin

Alvin was the brainchild—and namesake—of Allyn Vine, an oceanographer and submarine engineer at Woods Hole Oceanographic Institution (WHOI) in Woods Hole, Massachusetts. The craft itself was built by the mechanical division of General Mills (makers of the breakfast cereal Wheaties). The original *Alvin*, as launched in 1964, looked like nothing so much as a child's bathtub toy—a plump little white submarine. But *Alvin* could do things no other underwater vehicle in the world could, and over its long career it would be modified, updated, and overhauled to constantly expand and improve upon its capabilities.

Eventually, *Alvin*, as it performs today, would be equipped with a life-support system that could maintain three passengers for 80 hours; grasping pincers and a sample net and tray; sonar and a precision depth-finding system; a tracking beacon; a current meter; rear and front movable closed-circuit cameras and screen; a Plexiglas runner that allowed it to literally ski across the ocean floor (where suitable); a titanium passenger sphere and Plexiglas windows that doubled *Alvin*'s depth capabilities and could not be pierced by ill-tempered swordfish or marlin (which tilted at the vehicle on numerous occasions, causing considerable damage; surly squid were another problem entirely); thallium iodide searchlights that could illuminate the murky deeps; an oil-and-titanium steel-ball ballast system; and three motors for propulsion. Thus equipped, maintained and piloted by a somewhat eccentric but obsessively dedicated and fearless crew, and transported to virtually anyplace on the world's seas and oceans by its

The deep diving submersible Alvin, *the most productive of all the world's underwater research vessels. During its long career, which began in 1964,* Alvin, *a joint project of the U.S. Office of Naval Research and the Woods Hole Oceanographic Institution, has done everything from retrieving lost hydrogen bombs to exploring the wreck of the Titanic to examining ocean floor volcanic activity, mountain ranges, and hydrothermal vents.*

Although Alvin is nonthreatening in appearance to humans, marine life-forms ocasionally took exception to its presence. In 1967 this swordfish took a run at the submersible with enough force to imbed its sword in a seam in the vehicle. The irate fish narrowly missed one of the craft's viewports. Giant squid in particular also seemed to resent Alvin.

mother ship *Lulu, Alvin,* over the next 30 years, would become the faithful deep-water workhorse, or perhaps seahorse, of oceanographers, marine biologists, geologists, geophysicists, chemists, hydrographers, environmental

agencies, the U.S. government, and just about anyone else
who required its unique services.

And *Alvin* had barely completed its first test dives when
its services were required on a rather urgent matter by the

Alvin is prepared for a dive during the hunt for a hydrogen bomb that fell from a damaged B-52 into the Mediterranean, just off the Spanish village of Palomares in January 1966. Alvin's pilots located the device on a steep, muddy slope and then spent weeks relocating and chasing the recalcitrant bomb as it gradually slid down the incline and buried itself in the sea-floor ooze, as if it were reluctant to be recovered.

U.S. government. On January 17, 1966, a U.S. Air Force B-52 caught fire and exploded over Spain's Atlantic coast. One of the hydrogen bombs carried by the B-52 plunged into the Mediterranean Sea off the small fishing village of Palomares. The bomb was hundreds of times as powerful as the devices that destroyed Nagasaki and Hiroshima.

According to the Pentagon, the hydrogen bomb was unarmed. Nevertheless, its triggering mechanism packed a hefty charge of dynamite, and if the bomb's shell had cracked, which was likely, it would be leaking large amounts of high-level radiation into the Mediterranean— a nightmarish scenario. The navy was charged with the task of finding the thing, and they were quickly forced to admit

that there was only one vehicle they knew of that could accomplish such a task. This was particularly galling to navy officials, most of whom traditionally scoffed at the usefulness of submersibles. Now they had no choice but to send for *Alvin*.

The search for the missing H-bomb was one of the more harrowing episodes in *Alvin*'s career. The seafloor in that area was extremely murky, and visibility was rendered virtually nil in muddy areas, where *Alvin* itself churned up clouds of sediment. The currents were tricky, and the sea-bottom terrain was tortuous, with gullies, ridges, sudden drop-offs, and minor seamounts that seemed to loom up out of nowhere. To make matters worse, storms rolled up, which made it extremely difficult and dangerous for *Lulu* to deploy and retrieve the submersible, a touch-and-go operation even in mild seas. (Two years later, *Alvin*, its hatch open, would slip from *Lulu*'s deck and sink into the Atlantic during deployment, very nearly taking its crew with it. It would take 10 months to locate and retrieve the lost submersible.) Tensions between naval personnel and the unruly *Alvin* crew, who were fiercely protective of their craft, ran high. And there was the specter of the bomb itself, perhaps dangerously unstable and highly radioactive, most likely stuck halfway into the ooze and partially concealed on the floor of the Mediterranean.

Nevertheless, during its tenth dive, on March 1, *Alvin* discovered the track left in the seafloor by the sliding bomb. *Alvin*'s pilots followed the track as if they were hunting some sea monster to its lair. During *Alvin*'s 19th dive, on March 15, the monster itself was sighted. "What a big bastard," *Alvin* pilot Marvin McCamis commented. Photos were taken of the location, and *Alvin* surfaced. During the following dive, they could not relocate the tracks or the bomb. Once they found the tracks again, they saw that the bomb itself had slid down a gully. Finally, they relocated it. While waiting for the arrival of the navy ship that would actually hoist the bomb to the surface—the little *Alvin* could not budge the object—the bomb was lost again as it rolled farther down the gully. "Sir, this is dumb as hell," a naval officer commented in frustration to one of his superiors on the tracking vessel above. *Alvin's* pilots began to feel as if the bomb were deliberately eluding them.

As if it were a prize fish, American and Spanish military officials pose inanely with the lost hydrogen bomb after it was recovered from the floor of the Mediterranean. Alvin's pilots pinpointed the bomb's final resting place after 76 days of perilous dives.

During the next dive, with the hoisting ship in place, McCamis again located the bomb and, to the horror of his copilot, set *Alvin* right down on top of it, like a duck on a giant egg. Radioactivity or not, the pilot did not intend to lose it again. If it slid, he intended to slide right along with it. And there they waited until the bomb was secured and

winched to the surface from above, surely the most dangerous object ever dredged from the seabed.

During the following years, *Alvin* was used for less volatile missions. Marine biologists, geologists, geophysicists, and hydrographers were taken into the deeps for research, experimentation, and observation regarding everything from deep-water currents to plate tectonics to ocean-floor life-forms. They descended into deep trenches and troughs and climbed up and down towering seamounts. One of the most exciting series of dives occurred in March 1974, when *Alvin* carried a team of geologists into a rift valley in a section of the Mid-Ocean Range, about 400 miles off the Azores. There, among the towering seamounts of the earth's greatest mountain range, they examined underwater volcanoes, hovered over lava vents in the seafloor crust, and followed a seam between two sliding tectonic plates. The geologists were glued to the windows. "Your eye," commented one of the scientists on the unearthly scenery and the immense tectonic forces visibly at play, "does not believe it."

Alvin's most productive and spectacular mission, a series of dives that would revolutionize marine biology and geophysics and, indeed, shake the world scientific community as a whole, occurred during February and March 1977, and then again in 1979, when the submersible was contracted by the National Science Foundation to locate and explore hydrothermal vents in the floor of the Pacific. The vents, which were believed to be hot-water springs that emanated from cracks in the ocean floor along sliding tectonic plates and ejected rich deposits of metals, chemicals, and minerals from the earth's interior into the oceans, were still, among most marine geophysicists, a hypothetical concept. The series of dives made by *Alvin* to the tectonic seams on the floor of the Pacific, 200 miles off the Galápagos Islands, not only proved that the vents were a reality but initiated an entire new branch of marine biology and geophysics.

Most of the geophysicists who rode in *Alvin* during the first Pacific dives expected to find something, probably mineral-rich ocean-floor springs of a slightly higher water temperature than was usual for those extreme depths. Instead, *Alvin* descended into what one witness described as a "wonderland" of cathedral-like lava formations; bizarre-colored hills and ridges of mineral deposits; and geothermal vents releasing springs of unheard-of temperatures—over one vent, the water temperature was 662 degrees Fahrenheit, hot enough to melt and fuse components on the exterior of *Alvin*. Some vents, apparently releasing superheated, mineral-laden water from deep beneath the very mantle of the earth, belched what looked like thick white-and-black smoke. Although no sunlight penetrated these depths, the entire area seemed to shimmer. The geophysicists were stunned. "It altered my view of the world profoundly," one said. "I shall never forget it."

But the real surprise was waiting for the marine biologists. The first hint of the extraordinary things to come occurred as *Alvin* maneuvered in close to one of the vents for the first time. Jack Corliss, an oceanographer from Oregon State University who had come to study the vents, was aboard. As *Alvin* approached the vent, Corliss commented innocently over the radio to a graduate student who had accompanied him and who was monitoring the dive from the *Lulu*: "Debra, isn't the deep ocean supposed to be like a desert?" "Yes," replied Debra Stakes. "Well," Corliss continued, "there's all these animals down here . . . "

"All these animals down here . . . " Had a marine biologist been around to hear that remark, he or she might have fallen overboard in shock. Marine biologists since the days of the *Trieste*'s Mariana Trench dive knew that life could be found at even the deepest parts of the ocean, but at the depths of the vents, it had always proven to be extremely scarce and usually not actually indigenous to those depths. What Corliss and the *Alvin* pilot saw as they neared and then hovered over the vent was what they later described as a "jungle" of the strangest-looking creatures they had ever seen. Not being marine biologists themselves, they had no idea that these creatures had never been seen by *anyone* before.

When word of the discovery of marine life thriving around the geothermal vents got out, it did not take long for marine biologists from institutions around the country to begin requesting dives. What they saw at the vents was startling, to say the least. The vents were like watering holes in an African desert; marine life was abundant there. Indeed, it seemed like marine life actually grew and thrived there. And, as the biologists realized immediately, these life-forms could not be found in any marine-biology textbooks then in existence.

Stunned into silence, the biologists stared out *Alvin*'s windows at a bizarre scene. There were creatures that looked like dandelions; tangled clumps of stringlike animals that the *Alvin*'s crew referred to as "spaghetti," for want of a better description; "gardens" of tall white wormlike things that stood straight from the ocean floor; pink fish with startling blue eyes; giant white clams; segmented worms; an organism that looked like an "undulating hairbrush"; thousands of translucent anemones; a crustacean with teeth, instead of eyes, at the tips of its eye stalks; a variety of never-before-seen bioluminescent, gelatinous entities; and, the favorites of the *Alvin* pilots, hoards of large, spiderlike white crabs that scrambled about continuously, hopping and leaping all over the submarine and often clinging to it as it rose to the surface after a dive.

Dangling its pincers, sampling basket, and a newly developed vacuum hose, *Alvin* collected specimens by the thousands. The geothermal vents were a marine biologist's dream—an entirely new and unexpected ecosystem of creatures that apparently were part of a chemosynthetic, rather than a photosynthetic, life chain. Up until the discovery of geothermal life, science, for the most part, had

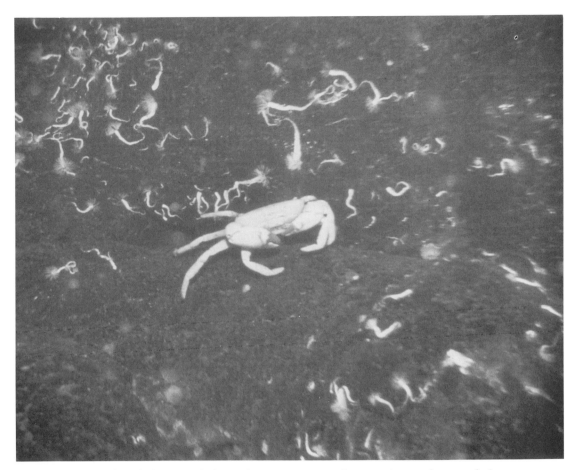

not even considered the possibility of an ecosystem that did not depend on sunlight and photosynthesis. This concept was something that was only discussed when the possibility of life on other planets came up. "This is a once-in-a-century finding, this, here on earth," one marine biologist commented. "There were people who saw Nobel prizes out there." Another scientist wrote: "Few discoveries in science come entirely unexpected. This is one of them."

Following the Galápagos vent dives, a few coveted hours in *Alvin* became the ultimate experience for marine biologists, chemists, and geophysicists. Throughout the 1980s, *Alvin* and its crew obliged them as best they could and during the following years made a seemingly endless

(continued on page 102)

Among the never-before-seen life-forms discovered at the Galápagos geothermal vents were multitudes of white, spiderlike crabs, whose madcap antics delighted Alvin's pilots. The creatures were a new, blind species of brachyuran crab.

Here There Be Monsters

As late as 1770, it was believed that life in the ocean did not exist beyond a depth of 1,800 feet. This theory was disproved in the early 19th century when the British nautical explorer James Clark Ross brought up marine life from depths of over 2,400 feet in Antarctic waters. The dredging expeditions of ships dispatched by Matthew Fontaine Maury in the mid-19th century and the historic *Challenger* expedition, launched in 1872, showed that animal life existed even in the deepest parts of the oceans and seas, although it was generally agreed that as the waters became deeper, darker, and colder, life-forms became increasingly scarce. Nevertheless, as the 1960 descent of the bathyscaphe *Trieste* in the Mariana Trench revealed, ocean life might be encountered at even the deepest, most sun-deprived place on the planet.

Today it is known that marine life-forms exist and vary in a strata of abundance and type as depth and water temperature change. The upper, or photic, zone, well lighted and relatively well heated by the sun, reaches down to about 700 feet below the surface. Here, the biomass is profuse and varied, and organisms from the tiny phytoplankton and zooplankton, which form the essential nutrient source for the food chain of the oceans and seas, to sardines, marlin, dolphin, tuna, gray sharks, and great white sharks thrive. Some inhabitants of the photic zone, such as the sperm whale, also spend much time in the mesopelagic zone, which extends downward about another 1,000 feet and is actually the shadowy, cooler, lower end of the photic zone, where squid and octopi are most at home.

At about 2,000 feet below the surface, the bathypelagic zone begins. Here, sunlight and warmth fade, and below this level life-forms become strange; it is the realm of sea monsters. Passengers in a submersible traveling through this eerie realm might glimpse in the vehicle's searchlights a 40-foot-long or 50-foot-long giant squid or a prehistoric coelacanth or deep-sea angler with its gaping, toothy mouth and glowing light at the end of a stalk protruding from its head. At about 3,500 feet below the surface the utterly sunless desert of the benthic zone begins. In the benthic cold and dark, life-forms are usually few and far between. Life in the benthic zone is rare as a general rule, but the hot geothermal vents such as those explored by *Alvin* in the Pacific off the Galápagos Islands provide an extraordinary exception.

In the boiling, mineral-rich oases produced by ocean-bottom tectonic activity, bizarre life-forms abound in an almost frightening profusion. Some benthic creatures, such as the luminous shark, bear a passing resemblance to their cousins from the upper levels, but most look like creatures from science fiction or horror movies. Many are bioluminescent, glowing with their own strange light. Others lack eyes, having adapted to the perpetual night in a manner that rendered visual organs unnecessary; thus they forfeited them to evolution centuries ago. Benthic creatures often resemble plants rather than animals, and some, as the crew of *Alvin* discovered, defy description altogether. They exhibit unique and startling means of feeding, reproduction, and self-propulsion. These animals are so far from the established biological and behavioral norms that they have forced marine biologists, zoologists, and other scientists to completely reconsider the concept of animal life on this planet.

The common octopus (Octopus vulgaris), despite its daunting appearance, is actually a timid, noncombative creature that inhabits nooks and cracks in cliffs and rock formations is the cool, shadowy mesopelagic depths. Underwater, octopi move with a graceful swiftness and flexibility. There is no record of an octopus ever attacking a human.

(continued from page 99)

succession of dives in waters around the world. Indeed, the
pilots were more than obliging, and there were numerous
close calls as *Alvin* dropped into the very mouths of active
underwater volcanoes on the East Pacific Rise and off the
Mariana Islands, maneuvered deftly through forests of
towering sulfide-deposit formations on the floor of the
Guaymas Basin, 400 miles out from the Gulf of California,
and pursued gelatinous zooplankton and siphonophores
(long chains or clumps of interdependent creatures) in the
Atlantic, off the coast of New York. *Alvin* even set down
on the corroded bridge, and toured the empty hull, of the
sunken *Titanic* to film the ghostly remains of that most
notorious of ocean disasters. But the pilots were expert and
Alvin seemed blessed, and there were never any serious
accidents, a remarkable record for a deep-water craft as
active as *Alvin*.

And *Alvin* and its passengers continued to discover previously unknown marine life-forms in the deep ocean.
More than any other deep-sea exploring vehicle or technique, *Alvin* was responsible for the now-accepted
knowledge that the oceans of earth harbor more animal life
than any other environment; indeed, it is now known that
a square foot of geothermal vent water provides a home to
more different species of animals, and in greater number,
than a square mile of tropical rainforest. (During *Alvin's*
second series of dives to the Galápagos vents in 1979, more
than 65,000 life-forms were taken as samples.)

As biologists studied samples of these vent creatures in
laboratories, their true significance was discovered. All of
the species seemed to be old; many of the geothermal-vent
organisms were nothing short of ancient. The tube worms,
for example, have been around for more than 600 million
years, predating the dinosaurs. At the bottom of the
geothermal food chain, it was learned, are vent microbes
called archaebacteria, the most ancient organisms on
earth. They cover the rocks and molten outcroppings of
the vents like a carpet. Thus, argue some marine biologists,

life on earth started at the geothermal vents some 4 billion years ago, with the archaebacteria at the bottom of the first food chain and the evolutionary ladder. If this hypothesis is correct, it could be said, in a sense, that *Alvin* and its crew had finally discovered, deep on the ocean floor, the cradle of life on this planet—the true *bathybius*.

Further Reading

Beach, Edward L. *Man Beneath the Sea: Exploring the Ocean World*. New York: Thomas Crowell, 1969.

Better, Albert. *The Discovery of the World*. New York: Simon and Schuster, 1960.

Bullard, Fred M. *Volcanoes of the Earth*. Austin: University of Texas Press, 1976.

Cowen, Robert C. *Frontiers of the Sea: The Story of Oceanographic Exploration*. New York: Doubleday, 1960.

Deacon, G. E. R., ed. *Seas, Maps, and Men: An Atlas-History of Man's Exploration of the Oceans*. Garden City, NY: Doubleday, 1962.

Deacon, Margaret. *Scientists and the Sea 1650—1900: A Study of Marine Science*. New York: Academic Press, 1971.

Goetzmann, William H. *New Lands, New Men: America and the Second Great Age of Discovery*. New York: Viking, 1986.

Hough, Richard. *The Great War at Sea*. Oxford: Oxford University Press, 1983.

Kaharl, Victoria A. *Water Baby: The Story of Alvin*. New York: Oxford, 1990.

Lewis, Charles L. *Matthew Fontaine Maury*. Salem, NH: Ayer, Co., 1980.

Madsen, Axel. *Cousteau: An Unauthorized Biography*. New York: Beaufort Books, 1986.

Munson, Richard. *Cousteau: The Captain and His World*. New York: William Morrow, 1989.

Newby, Eric. *The World Atlas of Exploration*. New York: Crescent, 1975.

Schlee, Susan. *The Edge of an Unfamiliar World*. New York: Dutton, 1973.

Shenton, Edward H. *Exploring the Ocean Depths*. New York: Norton, 1968.

————. *Diving for Science*. New York: Norton, 1972.

Tharp, Marie. *The Ocean Floor*. New York: John Wiley, 1982.

Urick, Robert J. *Principles of Underwater Sound*. New York: McGraw-Hill, 1983.

Chronology

1620   Dutchman Cornelis Drebbel builds the first operative submarine

1825   Matthew Fontaine Maury joins the U.S. Navy

1834   Maury's article, "On the Navigation of Cape Horn" is published in the *American Journal of Science and Arts*; Maury's *A New Theoretical and Practical Treatise on Navigation* is published

1849   Maury launches the first oceanographic research vessel, the USS *Taney*

1855   Maury's *The Physical Geography of the Sea* is published

1858   The laying of the first transatlantic telegraph cable begins

1870   Jules Verne's *Twenty Thousand Leagues Under the Sea* is published

1872   The British launch the HMS *Challenger* on the most ambitious oceanographic expedition to date

1934   Charles William Beebe descends farther into the ocean depths in his bathysphere than anyone before him

1937   Auguste Piccard begins constructing a bathyscaphe, later named the *Trieste*

1954   The U.S. Navy launches the first nuclear submarine, the *Nautilus*

1958   The *Nautilus* is piloted under the North Pole by Captain William Anderson

1960   Jacques Piccard and Don Walsh descend into the Mariana Trench in the *Trieste*

1963   The USS *Thresher* nuclear submarine mysteriously disappears off the coast of Massachusetts during a deep-sea dive

1964   The mobile deep-sea submersible *Alvin* is launched

1967   *Alvin* aids the U.S. military in the recovery of a submerged hydrogen bomb in the Mediterranean

1977   *Alvin* locates and explores hydrothermal vents in the floor of the Pacific

1979   *Alvin* returns to the hydrothermal vents for further exploration

Index

Picture Credits

AP/Wide World Photos: pp. 57, 76, 78–79, 80, 83, 86, 88; Aquarium for Wildlife Conservation: p. 101; The Bettmann Archive: pp. 19, 35, 52–53; Nautilus Memorial, Submarine Force Library and Museum: pp. 48, 59, 60–61, 62; Report of the Scientific Results of HMS *Challenger*, by Great Britain–Challenger office/General Research Division, New York Public Library, Astor, Lenox and Tilden Foundations: pp. 32, 36, 38, 40–41, 42, 43, 44; *Explanations and Sailing Directions To Accompany the Wind and Current Charts*, by Matthew Fontaine Maury/General Research Division, New York Public Library, Astor, Lenox and Tilden Foundations: pp. 24, 26, 28–29; Reproduced by permission of Marie Tharp, 1 Washington Avenue, South Nyack, NY: cover map; UPI/Bettmann: p. 85; U.S. Naval Historical Center, Washington Navy Yard: pp. 12, 16–17, 22–23, 73; U.S. Naval Institute, Annapolis: pp. 74, 92; U.S. Navy: pp. 54, 94–95; *20,000 Leagues under the Sea*, by Jules Verne/General Research Division, New York Public Library, Astor, Lenox and Tilden Foundations: p. 51; Woods Hole Oceanographic Institution: pp. 65 (Jack White-head), 66 (Rod Catanach), cover inset, 67 (Robert Ballard), 68, 69 (J. Frederick Grassle), 70 (Dr. Robert Hessler, SIO), 71 (John Edmond, MIT), 72 (Mitchell Lyle, OSU), 90–91, 99 (John B. Corliss).

Richard Gaines graduated from the University of Texas with a B.A. in English and an M.A. in Library Science.

William H. Goetzmann holds the Jack S. Blanton, Sr., Chair in History at the University of Texas at Austin, where he has taught for many years. The author of numerous works on American history and exploration, he won the 1967 Pulitzer and Parkman prizes for his *Exploration and Empire: The Role of the Explorer and Scientist in the Winning of the American West, 1800–1900.* With his son William N. Goetzmann, he coauthored *The West of the Imagination,* which received the Carr P. Collins Award in 1986 from the Texas Institute of Letters. His documentary television series of the same name received a blue ribbon in the history category at the American Film and Video Festival held in New York City in 1987. A recent work, *New Lands, New Men: America and the Second Great Age of Discovery,* was published in 1986 to much critical acclaim.

Michael Collins served as command module pilot on the *Apollo 11* space mission, which landed his colleagues Neil Armstrong and Buzz Aldrin on the moon. A graduate of the United States Military Academy, Collins was named an astronaut in 1963. In 1966 he piloted the *Gemini 10* mission, during which he became the third American to walk in space. The author of several books on space exploration, Collins was director of the Smithsonian Institution's National Air and Space Museum from 1971 to 1978 and is a recipient of the Presidential Medal of Freedom.